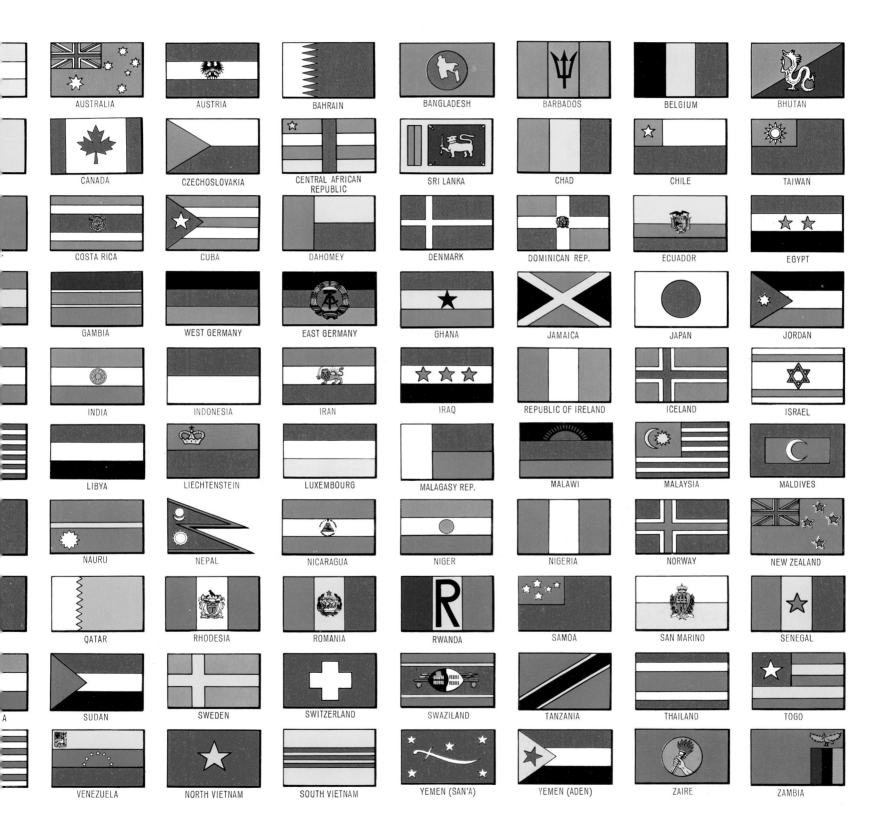

AUSTRALIA	AUSTRIA	BAHRAIN	BANGLADESH	BARBADOS	BELGIUM	BHUTAN
CANADA	CZECHOSLOVAKIA	CENTRAL AFRICAN REPUBLIC	SRI LANKA	CHAD	CHILE	TAIWAN
COSTA RICA	CUBA	DAHOMEY	DENMARK	DOMINICAN REP.	ECUADOR	EGYPT
GAMBIA	WEST GERMANY	EAST GERMANY	GHANA	JAMAICA	JAPAN	JORDAN
INDIA	INDONESIA	IRAN	IRAQ	REPUBLIC OF IRELAND	ICELAND	ISRAEL
LIBYA	LIECHTENSTEIN	LUXEMBOURG	MALAGASY REP.	MALAWI	MALAYSIA	MALDIVES
NAURU	NEPAL	NICARAGUA	NIGER	NIGERIA	NORWAY	NEW ZEALAND
QATAR	RHODESIA	ROMANIA	RWANDA	SAMOA	SAN MARINO	SENEGAL
SUDAN	SWEDEN	SWITZERLAND	SWAZILAND	TANZANIA	THAILAND	TOGO
VENEZUELA	NORTH VIETNAM	SOUTH VIETNAM	YEMEN (SAN'A)	YEMEN (ADEN)	ZAIRE	ZAMBIA

SBN 361 03369 9 © 1973 Vallardi Industrie Grafiche Published 1976 by Purnell Books, Berkshire House, Queen Street, Maidenhead, Berkshire ©1976 Purnell and Sons Limited

Purnell's Illustrated
World Atlas

Edited by Chris Tunney

PURNELL

COUNTRIES OF THE WORLD

There are more than 150 independent countries in the world, and their number is increasing all the time. Some colonies win their independence, as, for example, Papua New Guinea did in 1975; some countries are partitioned as the result of internal conflict, as was Pakistan, when the Eastern Province broke away to form the independent nation of Bangladesh in 1971; and some new countries are formed by the amalgamation of a number of countries into a union, as was the case with the United Arab Emirates, formed by the union of seven small states in 1971.

One country differs from another in a number of ways, and one of the most apparent is its land area. Among the smallest countries on this basis are Vatican City, with an area of only a sixth of a square mile (0.44 sq km), and Monaco (0.7 sq mile or 1.8 sq km). The largest is the USSR, which covers an area of 8,650,000 sq miles (22,403,000 sq km) and is more than twice as large as the next two countries, Canada and the United States. The populations of countries also vary widely. The most populous are China, with some 800 million inhabitants, India (593 million), the USSR (238 million), and the United States (210 million), and these figures are increasing all the time. Countries with very low populations include Vatican City (1,000), Nauru (7,000), and Andorra (25,000). If we compare the area of a country with its population, we may calculate its population density. The country with the lowest density is Mongolia, with 2.3 persons per square mile (0.9/sq km). Botswana, Libya, and Mauritania all have about 3 persons per square mile (1.2/sq km), and Australia's population density is only 4.4 per square mile (1.7/sq km). The countries with the greatest densities of population are those that consist of little more than a single town, such as Monaco (33,000/sq mile or 12,800/sq km) and Singapore (9,820/sq mile or 3,793/sq km).

Countries are further differentiated from one another by a large number of geographical, economic, social, and cultural conditions, such as the excess or shortage of water, the extent and productivity of the arable land, and everything that man by his labours has made out of the natural resources.

EEC (European Economic Community) was founded in 1957 by six nations: Belgium, France, Italy, Luxembourg, the Netherlands, and West Germany. Denmark, Great Britain, and the Republic of Ireland joined in 1972. The object of the Treaty of Rome, which set up the EEC, was to lay the foundations of an enduring and closer union between the European peoples, in particular by establishing a common market without trade barriers. Economic and monetary union was planned to take effect by 1980. Political union is proceeding with caution. The member countries have a total of 253 million people.

OAU (Organization of African Unity), established at Addis Ababa in 1963 when the heads of 30 African states signed the Charter of African Unity, now encompasses more than 40 independent African nations. The charter's stated aims are to promote solidarity and co-operation, to defend the independence of African states, and to remove all forms of colonialism from Africa. The OAU supports the freedom movements of those African peoples who are not yet independent. The OAU countries have a combined 320 million inhabitants.

COMECON (or CMEA, the Council for Mutual Economic Assistance) was founded in 1949 by six Eastern Bloc countries, the USSR, Bulgaria, Czechoslovakia, Hungary, Poland, and Romania. Other countries admitted later were Albania (who ceased participation), Cuba, East Germany, and Mongolia. Yugoslavia enjoys associate status, and China, North Korea, and North Vietnam are observers. The purpose of the union is common economic planning, the exchange of scientific and technical knowhow, and a steady advance of the welfare of the peoples. There are 350 million people living in the COMECON countries.

LAFTA (Latin American Free Trade Association) came about in 1960 through the Treaty of Montevideo. The agreement was signed by Argentina, Brazil, Chile, Mexico, Paraguay, Peru, and Uruguay. Colombia, Ecuador, Venezuela, and Bolivia joined later. Formerly these countries conducted only 10-12 per cent of their external trade with each other. LAFTA was set up to increase the mutual exchange of goods and gradually abolish customs barriers. The total population of LAFTA countries is 238 million.

Europe *Area 4,036,000 sq miles (10,454,000 sq km); population 650,000,000; population density 161 persons per sq mile (62/sq km).* Europe has been favoured by its situation in the Temperate Zone. As a result, it was quickly colonized and acquired cultural traditions going a long way back in history. After the Dark Ages, science and technology grew apace. Europeans explored and conquered nearly all the other continents.

Asia *Area 17,328,000 sq miles (44,879,000 sq km); population 2,224,000,000; population density 128 persons per sq mile (50/sq km).* The largest of the continents, Asia has widely varying climates. There are both intensely humid and intensely dry regions, and also the highest mountain peaks in the world. Some 58 per cent of the world's people live in Asia. Much of the population live in considerable poverty, but industrial development is widespread.

Africa *Area 11,700,000 sq miles (30,300,000 sq km); population 391,000,000; population density 33 persons per sq mile (13/sq km).* Apart from the Egyptians, the Berbers, and the Ethiopians, the native population of Africa is Negroid. Most of the north is desert (the Sahara), and on the equator there are huge tropical rain forests. The continent has been developed but often exploited by Europeans since the 1500s, and the peoples are still very impoverished.

North & Central America *Area 9,363,000 sq miles (24,250,000 sq km); population 320,000,000; population density 34 persons per sq mile (13/sq km).* The continent that encompasses North and Central America is largely characterized by broad landscapes with extensive agriculture and rich mineral resources. The population consists, in the main, of the descendants of European immigrants. The original inhabitants, the Amerindians, are today a small minority.

South America *Area 6,873,000 sq miles (17,800,000 sq km); population 192,000,000; population density 28 persons per sq mile (11/sq km).* The continent is traversed by the high mountain range of the Andes. In the Amazon Basin, there are huge rain forests. The northern part of the continent lies on the equator, whereas the southern part stretches into Antarctica. The Spaniards and Portuguese settled in the land and exploited it. Much of the population live in poverty.

Oceania *Area 3,286,000 sq miles (8,511,000 sq km); population 20,000,000; population density 6 persons per sq mile (2.3/sq km).* The continent known as Oceania includes Australia, New Zealand, and Papua New Guinea, and some 30,000 Pacific islands. The islands are inhabited largely by the original native peoples. Australia and New Zealand are peopled mainly by European immigrants and their descendants, and have some 80 per cent of the population of Oceania.

EUROPE

GREECE—The island of Aegina, with the ruins of the Temple of Aphaia

Europe, with an area of some 4 million square miles (10 million sq km), is the second smallest of the continents—only Australia is smaller. A look at the map on pages 10 and 11 shows that Europe forms a single land mass with the huge continent of Asia. The border between them is formed by the Ural Mountains, the River Ural, the lowlands extending from the Caspian Sea to the Black Sea, the Bosporus, the Sea of Marmora, and the Dardanelles. As Europe and Asia merge into each other in this way, geographers often refer to the combined land mass of the two continents as *Eurasia*.

In eastern Europe a huge lowland area stretches in the south as far as the Carpathian Mountains and the Balkans. A fertile low plain spreads over northern Germany and the Netherlands, stretching across France as far as the Bay of Biscay and the

Pyrenees. The north of Europe is mountainous, with ranges extending from Scandinavia to Scotland and Ireland. The lowland areas are continued in a southerly direction in central and western Europe, as also in the west of eastern Europe, by a region of alternating highlands and broad valleys. The mighty mountain ranges of the Alps and Pyrenees constitute the boundary between central and southern Europe. The southern edge of the continent is particularly rich in peninsulas and islands, and it is also traversed by highland regions.

Both the geographical situation and the shape of Europe have proved extremely favourable to its inhabitants throughout the ages. Europe lies in the temperate climatic zone. The north-west benefits from the warming influence of the Gulf Stream. And the westerly drift of the winds brings with it

abundant precipitation from the nearby Atlantic Ocean. The deeply indented coastlines, with the arms of the sea reaching far inland, also help the climate.

The origins of the European family of peoples are still obscure to scholars. Certainly, they lie far back in the mists of antiquity. We know that most European languages of today are interconnected, and that they have a relationship with the Sanskrit of India. Language researchers are forever seeking the basic Indo-European language that was the parent of all the others, and at the same time trying to identify the original homeland of the Indo-European peoples. It may be that this lay in the Near East, or perhaps in the land between the Rhine and the Volga.

No-one knows where the name 'Europe' comes from. Perhaps the Assyrians gave us the word, designating as 'Ereb' the 'land of darkness 'that lay to the west of their own country. The Ancient Greeks told of Europa, the daughter of a legendary king.

Europe was not the cradle of mankind, but it was colonized very early in history. The tribes living there in the Old Stone Age led a hard, nomadic life. They started cultivating the land in the New Stone Age, and as a result they began to settle and form communities.

The land connection with Asia and the narrows of the Bosporus and Strait of Gibraltar facilitated the movements of the tribes. Both warlike conflicts and peaceful penetration throughout thousands of years eventually produced the multiplicity and distinctive character of the European peoples.

At the beginning of the modern era, the maritime nations of Europe sailed far beyond their own frontiers. They discovered and conquered whole continents. The Russians pushed eastwards as far as the Pacific Ocean, thus extending their domain deep into Asia.

Europe became rich, its prosperity in no small part due to the enslavement of whole peoples and the plundering of their natural resources. At the same time, however, the achievements of European science and technology have redounded to the benefit of many of the world's peoples.

ICELAND *Area 39,709 sq miles (102,846 sq km); population 210,000; capital, Reykjavik (pop. 84,000); currency, króna (100 aurar); official language, Icelandic.*

Iceland formerly belonged to Denmark, but became an independent kingdom in 1918 and then, in 1944, a republic. Most of the ground consists of solid lava, and there are still a few volcanic vents. Little land is left that can be used for agriculture. The most important source of revenue is fishing. The houses are heated by the numerous hot springs.

IRELAND, REPUBLIC OF *Area 27,135 sq miles (70,279 sq km); population 2,971,000; capital, Dublin (pop. 566,000); currency, pound (100 pence); official languages, English and Gaelic.*

Ireland lies west of Great Britain, across the Irish Sea, and consists of the Republic of Ireland, which has been independent since 1948, and the north-eastern part, Northern Ireland, which is part of the United Kingdom. There is an extensive flat stretch of land with lakes, bordered on north and south by highland country. Ireland is called the 'Emerald Isle' because of its lush pastures—the essential raw material for the prosperous cattle rearing industry. The main agricultural product are cereals and potatoes. The manufacture of foodstuffs is an important industry.

ITALY *Area 116,303 sq miles (301,223 sq km); population 54,025,000; capital, Rome (pop. 2,843,000); currency, lira; official language, Italian.*

Italy as we know it today was not unified until 1861. It remained a monarchy until after World War II, when, in 1946, the people voted to make it a republic.

The Italian peninsula is bounded in the north by the Alps, and is traversed by the Apennines, running from north-west to southeast, for the whole of its length. In the north, south of the Alps, the fertile plain of the Po stretches to the Adriatic Sea.

The most important agricultural products are wheat, rice, maize, vegetables, olives,

Mont-Saint-Michel *(above)* lies in the Gulf of St Malo off the coast of Brittany, in north-east France, and is crowned by a famous abbey. The place owes its fame to a peculiar phenomenon: when the tide rises, the mount becomes an island, but at low tide land communication with the mainland is re-established. The extent of ebb and flow of the tides varies from coast to coast. On the Atlantic coast, for example, the water level at high tide rises an average of 10-16 feet (3-5 metres), and at St Malo as much as 40 feet (12 metres). It is not surprising that this is the site of the first tidal power station in the world.

Below: Windmills at Kinderyk, in the Netherlands. There are still a thousand or so windmills in the Netherlands. They formerly served to produce power for removing water, but have now become merely a symbol of the country. Most have now been replaced by electric motors. The country is noted for its peaceable acquisition of land. New land has been reclaimed from the sea by the building of numerous dams.

Left: Grand' Place, Brussels, Belgium. Brussels, the capital, is in the centre of the country. The town, which dates from the 6th century, contains fine examples of both medieval and modern architecture. The industrial quarters are on the outskirts of the town. Of the many buildings of artistic interest, the Grand' Place is particularly noteworthy, with its medieval guildhouses and famous old town hall, the most impressive Gothic building in the capital. After World War II, Brussels became a modern metropolis, in which important international organizations, such as the European Economic Community, have their headquarters.

The Eiffel Tower *(left)* was built in 1889 for the Paris World Fair, to demonstrate to visitors from all over the world that France had become an industrial power. This structure symbolizes an epoch, marked by unprecedented scientific and technological progress, in which the most important inventions of the Industrial Age—the incandescent lamp, telephone, steam-engine, and electric motor—were achieved. The wrought-iron tower rises 984 feet (300 metres) into the sky, a landmark for every visitor to Paris. Lifts and stairs lead to the three platforms, which provide a majestic view of the French capital. Paris is one of the most beautiful towns in the world, having played a highly significant role in European history.

Below: London, the Houses of Parliament. In both area and population, London is the largest city in Europe. It is situated on the Thames, the most important river in England, which connects the capital with the sea by a broad estuary. London has been a prosperous centre of trade since the Middle Ages, and has continued to grow. It has a wealth of history, and its famous buildings include: Westminster Abbey, with its Royal Tombs; The Tower of London, a 900-year-old fortress on the Thames, which amongst other things houses the Crown Jewels; St Paul's Cathedral, built by Christopher Wren some 300 years ago; and the Houses of Parliament. This magnificent building on the banks of the Thames consists of the House of Lords and the House of Commons, and is also known as the Palace of Westminster. The clock tower is the famous Big Ben. The Houses of Parliament were erected in Neo-Gothic style during the reign of Queen Victoria in the mid-1800s.

citrus fruits, and the vine. Italy produces and exports more wine than any other country in the world.

There are abundant supplies of marble. Important industries include metal-working, mechanical engineering (especially motor-cars), the processing of foodstuffs, and oil refining. Tourism is a major source of revenue, for no other country in the world possesses so many ancient art treasures.

LIECHTENSTEIN *Area 62 sq miles (161 sq km); population 23,000; capital, Vaduz (pop. 4,000); currency, franc (Swiss); official language, German.*

Liechtenstein has been a hereditary principality since the 1340s, and became an independent state in 1719. It is a tiny country, consisting of nothing but mountains, between Austria and Switzerland. It is almost completely covered with forests.

LUXEMBOURG *Area 999 sq miles (2,587 sq km); population 348,000; capital, Luxembourg (pop. 78,000); currency, franc (100 centimes); official languages, French, Luxembourgeois, and German.*

The Grand Duchy of Luxembourg has been independent since 1867. It is a hilly country, and potatoes, cereals, and fruit are cultivated. The main source of revenue comes from the mining of iron ore.

MALTA *Area 122 sq miles (316 sq km); population 322,000; capital, Valletta (pop. 16,000); currency, pound (100 cents); official languages, Maltese and English.*

An island in the middle of the Mediterranean to the south of Sicily, Malta (which also includes the smaller islands of Gozo and Comino) became an independent country in 1964, after 150 years of British rule. The island has a mountainous landscape. Cereals, vines, and vegetables are cultivated.

MONACO *Area 0·7 sq miles (1·8 sq km); population 23,000; capital, Monaco (pop. 2,000); currency, franc (French); official languages, French and Monégasque.*

This little principality lies on the French Mediterranean coast to the east of Nice. Its favourable climate and the well-known Monte Carlo casino attract many tourists.

NETHERLANDS *Area 13,500 sq miles (34,965 sq km); population 13,259,000; capital, Amsterdam (pop. 807,000); currency, guilder (100 cents); official language, Dutch.*

After a period of domination by France, the Netherlands became an independent constitutional monarchy in 1815. At that time it also included what are now Belgium (broke azay in 1830) and Luxembourg (1890).

The land is a plain, partly below sea level and protected by high dykes. The port of Rotterdam (pop. 654,000) has the largest turnover of merchandise in the world.

The marine climate brings heavy rainfall, and the fertile soil bears rich crops of vegetables, flowers, and potatoes. Cereals are grown principally as fodder for the abundant cattle, which produce milk and cheese. The foodstuffs processing industry is highly developed. There are large margarine factories, electrical engineering works, and petroleum refineries.

NORWAY *Area 125,181 sq miles (324,217 sq km); population 3,948,000; capital, Oslo (pop. 477,000); currency, krone (100 öre); official languages, Bokmål (or Riksmål) and Nynorsk (or Landsmål).*

Norway was at various times united with Denmark or Sweden, and has a monarchy that goes back a thousand years. Most of the country is mountainous, with deep fjords along the coast. The Gulf Stream provides a mild climate for the latitude, so that the ports remain free of ice throughout the winter. The most important economic activity is fishing. Huge pine forests provide wood for the paper industry. In the tundra of the far north, there are 22,000 nomadic Lapps, who keep reindeer. Hydraulic power is drawn from the numerous waterfalls, and these provide even the smallest villages with electricity. Iron ore is mined, and oil began to be extracted from the North Sea fields in the 1970s.

POLAND *Area 120,360 sq miles (311,730 sq km); population 32,889,000; capital, Warsaw (pop. 1,308,000); currency, zloty (100 groszy); official language, Polish.*

A People's Republic, Poland was once a monarchy, but its powerful neighbours several times forced it into accepting partial or total partitioning of its territory. After World War II, the victorious powers fixed Poland's new borders.

Most of Poland lies in the plain that stretches from Russia to northern Germany. Only towards the south does the land become at all mountainous. The most important economic activity is still agriculture, and the potato harvest is the second largest in the world. Cattle rearing provides meat exports as well as covering Poland's own needs. Silesia has rich mineral deposits, including coal, iron, lead, and zinc.

PORTUGAL *Area 34,240 sq miles (88,680 sq km); population 8,545,000; capital, Lisbon (pop. 783,000); currency, escudo (100 centavos); official language, Portuguese.*

Portugal was a monarchy until 1911, and has been an independent country since the 12th century. A military coup in 1974 saw the beginning of an internal struggle between various political factions.

The country occupies most of the western part of the Iberian Peninsula, and is traversed by mountain ranges and by rivers such as the Douro and Tagus (Tejo) that rise in Spain and flow into the Atlantic. Nearly half the people work on the land and in the forests. The mild climate is favourable to the cultivation of vegetables, cereal crops, olives, and, above all, the vine. Port, a fortified wine, is exported to countries all over the world. Fishing is an important industry, most of the catch (especially sardines and tuna) being canned. The harbour towns of Lisbon and Oporto have large industrial areas. Portugal has the most extensive cork forests in the world. The lovely coastline and picturesque forests attract large numbers of tourists.

ROMANIA *Area 91,700 sq miles (237,500 sq km); population 20,470,000; capital, Bucharest (pop. 1,488,000); currency, leu (100 bani); official language, Romanian.*

After being under Turkish control for a number of years, Romania became fully independent in 1878. It was a monarchy until 1947, and a year later a communist government was set up. The country is traversed by two crescent-shaped and wooded ranges of the Carpathians. Between them lies the Transylvanian plateau. The plains of Walachia and Moldavia extend towards the south and

Above: West Germany, the Rhine near Bacharach. The Rhine is the longest river in central Europe. Along its banks, huge industrial and commercial centres have arisen. It is connected by canal with numerous other rivers, including the Rhône, the Loire, the Seine, the Meuse, the Ems, the Weser, and the Elbe. By the early 1980s, the Rhine-Main-Danube Canal will also link the Rhine with the Black Sea. On these waterways, barges are used for a massive central European exchange of merchandise, in which Switzerland, France, Germany, the Netherlands, Belgium, and even countries overseas take part. The Rhine valley is particularly beautiful between Bingen and Koblenz, after the river has broken through the slate mountains—many vineyards and castles are to be seen along its banks.

Centre: Rothenburg ob der Tauber, West Germany. War and the growth of new towns have destroyed a large number of historical buildings in Germany. However, many of the smaller towns have managed to retain the beauty of their old quarters, and today still attract art-loving tourists.

Right: Fallow deer. The constant and irresistible march of industrialization threatens the natural scene in Germany, too. The first German wildlife protection park was set up on the Lüneburger Heath in 1956. Since then, more than 40 further nature parks have sprung into existence, totalling in area some 11,500 square miles (30,000 sq km). And in the remaining forest areas and open land there are strict hunting regulations, and the forester accepts his function as a warden and protector of the wildlife.

east, broken by the tributaries of the Danube and a number of lakes. In the south-east, the country reaches the Black Sea. Most workers are employed on the collective farms, but the country's main wealth stems predominantly from industry and mining. Romania is one of Europe's leading oil-producing countries.

SAN MARINO *Area 24 sq miles (62 sq km); population 19,000; capital, San Marino (pop. 2,000); currency, lira (Italian); official language, Italian.*

The independence of San Marino, the world's smallest republic, goes back to the 1200s, and it was founded about AD 350. Its status was recognized by Italy in 1862. Entirely surrounded by Italy, the country lies on the eastern slopes of the Apennines. The main sources of revenue are agriculture, stockbreeding, and tourism.

SPAIN *Area 194,885 sq miles (504,750 sq km); population 34,033,000; capital, Madrid (pop. 3,150,000); currency, peseta (100 céntimos); official language, Castilian Spanish (Basque, Catalan, and Galician are spoken in their respective regions).*

A monarchy for many centuries, Spain became a republic in 1931. After the parties of the left had been successful in the 1936 elections, civil war broke out. It lasted three years, and the victorious General Franco became head of state. In 1947, he declared that Spain would revert to a monarchy, which it did when he died 28 years later.

Spain has two large plains—the Ebro basin in Aragon and the dry basin of the Guadalquivir in lower Andalusia. The rest of the country is mountainous, with, in the centre, the largely rainless Meseta plateau, which covers three-quarters of the country. Cereal crops, vines and olives are grown there. A third of the work force is engaged in agriculture, either as labourers on private estates or as smallholders. One big problem is the migration of young people to the towns and tourist centres.

SWEDEN *Area 173,400 sq miles (449,110 sq km); population 8,115,000; capital, Stockholm (pop. 1,307,000); currency, krona (100 öre); official language, Swedish.*

The Swedish monarchy has existed for nearly a thousand years. For more than the last 150 of these, Sweden has been involved

Above: Granada, Spain. The town is situated in the foothills of the province of the same name. It was built on the slopes of three hills, and it is bordered on the south by the foothills of the Sierra Nevada. Granada was captured by the Arabs in AD 711, and then became the last stronghold of the Moorish kingdom in Spain. The Spaniards recaptured it in 1492. The architecture of the town bears a strong Arab stamp, and it still attracts thousands of tourists and is justly counted among the most picturesque sights of the Iberian Peninsula. It is still in part surrounded by the towers and walls dating from earlier periods. On one of its hills, the Alhambra palace and fortress was constructed to be the noble summer residence of its overlords, and this building is one of the most magnificent examples of Moorish art. The gardens that surround the building are also famous.

Below: Bullfighting in Spain. The bullfight is a typical Spanish spectacle. The law requires that the bulls must be between 4 and 5 years old, have no bodily defects, and their horns must be sharp. The bullfighters who have the job of inflicting on the bull the last, fatal blow are called *matadors.* Lots are cast to decide which bulls are assigned to which fighters. In the first phase, the bull is taunted by the *peons* with a red cloak and chased all round the arena. The second phase consists of a *picador* on horseback trying to ward off the charging bull by blows of a lance between the animal's shoulder-blades. It is then the turn of the three *banderiller–s,* who direct barbed, beribboned darts into the animal's neck. When the bull is then in an extreme state of excitement, the *torero* enters the arena with his long sword and further excites the bull with the red cloak attached to a stick. It is at this critical moment that he may succeed in killing the bull from the front with a blow between its shoulder-blades. If the bull merely falls to its knees, then the *matador* gives it the *coup de grâce.*

Right: Tuna fishing is extensively practised in the southern Mediterranean, and is an essential feature in the economy of the islands of Sicily and Sardinia. The net used for tuna fishing has a number of compartments, arranged vertically, into which the fish enter. The last of these compartments is called the 'death chamber'. When the fish have reached this point, the leader of the expedition gives the word of command for the net to be drawn in. The fish are dazed by their own threshing about and by the blows inflicted by the fishermen, and can easily be caught on hooks.

in no wars. The social welfare and schools systems are exemplary.

The eastern half of the Scandinavian mountain chain lies in Sweden. The land falls away gradually to the south-east until it reaches the Baltic. Numerous waterfalls are exploited for electric power. One-twelfth of the country is covered by lakes. In the plains, vast fields of wheat, sugar-beet, and potatoes are to be seen, and the forests of central Sweden provide immense quantities of timber. What is not exported is processed for furniture, cellulose, and paper. Sweden is a highly industrialized country, manufacturing, in particular, high-quality steel. Other important industries are shipbuilding, car and ball-bearing manufacture, and chemicals. The northern parts are peopled by several thousand Lapps, who live largely by rearing reindeer.

SWITZERLAND *Area 15,940 sq miles (41,284 sq km); population 6,270,000; capital, Bern (pop. 162,000); currency, franc (100 centimes); official languages, German, French, and Italian.*

The Federal Government consists of 22 basically independent *cantons,* whose parishes also enjoy the right to a considerable amount of self-administration. The country has been neutral for some 150 years. Sandwiched between Austria and France in one direction, and between Italy and West Germany in another, Switzerland lies squarely in the Alps, and half of the country is higher than 3,300 feet (1,000 metres). The northern part, the so-called *Mittelland* (the Swiss plateau), has a surface broken by many lakes and rivers. The main crop there is wheat, but on the mountain slopes cattle are reared and there is much dairy farming. Swiss industry is highly specialized, being concentrated on foodstuffs, pharmaceutical products, and precision engineering (especially watches and clocks). Tourism is very important.

UNITED KINGDOM *Area 94,216 sq miles (244,018 sq km); population 55,522,000; capital, London (pop. 7,379,000); currency, pound (100 pence); official language, English.*

The United Kingdom of Great Britain and Northern Ireland is governed by a system of parliamentary democracy. The country is generally hilly, and Scotland and Wales are mountainous. The rivers are not very long, but they are for the most part navigable. The climate tends to be unsettled. Britain imports much food, especially from its former colonies, which today belong to the Commonwealth, of which Britain is the head. Sheep rearing is an important industry, producing meat and wool. Fishing is also important, and coal and other minerals produce considerable revenue. It was in Britain that the Industrial Revolution began in the 18th century, and this led to economic prosperity—textiles, engineering, motor-car and aeroplane manufacturing, and shipbuilding. Britain has also played a leading role in the development of rail traffic, and its merchant navy is one of the finest in the world. The country's insular situation, its many excellent river ports, and its frontage on the Atlantic Ocean, have made of the British a nation of mariners. In the 1970s, Britain, with its dwindling prosperity and severe balance-of-trade deficits, saw a possible solution in the development of its considerable North Sea oil resources.

USSR (Russia) *Area 8,650,000 sq miles (22,403,000 sq km); in Europe, 2,150,000 sq miles (5,568,000 sq km); in Asia, 6,500,000 sq miles (16,835,000 sq km); population*

Above: Italy, the stark, stone peaks of the Sassolungo, in the Dolomites. The Italian landscape is extremely varied—picturesque, magnificent, friendly, rugged, or gracious, but seldom monotonous.

Right: Rome, the Piazza Navona, which dates from the 17th century. Apart from densely populated residential quarters and modern buildings, the city also contains impressive ruins from the time of the emperors and many magnificent churches, palaces, and fountains in Renaissance and baroque styles. Rome, which is rightly regarded as one of the most beautiful cities of the world, is not only the capital of Italy, it is also the centre of world Catholicism.

Below: Portovenere, with the island of Palmaria, an old outpost of Genoa. This is one of the innumerable beauty spots on the Italian Mediterranean coastline.

Above: The island of Mykonos, one of a group of Greek islands known as the Cyclades. The box-shaped houses, all whitewashed, are typical of the area. There are about 220 islands in the group, which lies in the south Aegean Sea, between the Peloponnesus and the Dodecanese.

Below: Red Square, Moscow, fringed by the walls of the Kremlin and by St Basil's Cathedral. The square dates back to the 15th century, but it was only about a hundred years ago that it began to look as it does today, with its towers, its domes, and its relics of an age-old history. Now it is the political centre of the giant state. The USSR stretches some 5,250 miles (8,450 km) at its greatest distance from west to east, i.e. more than a fifth of the earth's circumference.

238,371,000 (in Europe 179,407,000; in Asia 58,964,000); capital, Moscow (pop. 7,172,000); currency, rouble (100 copecks); official language, Russian.

The USSR (Union of Soviet Socialist Republics) is a multi-national state consisting of 15 Union Republics, 20 Autonomous Republics, 8 Autonomous Regions, and 10 National Areas. The 'Russians' themselves constitute the majority of the population. Originally the Russians lived only in the heartland of the Soviet Union, but now they are to be found all over, especially in Siberia. There are major distinctions between Great Russians, Little Russians (Ukrainians), and White Russians, but, apart from these, there are more than a hundred races: Uzbeks, Tartars, Armenians, Georgians, Turkomans, Kazakhs, and others, all with their own languages.

In area, the Soviet Union is the largest country in the world, occupying more than half the continent of Europe and about a third of Asia. The centre and north of the European part is tableland. In the south, the frontier is formed by the Caucasus Mountains. The Volga is the longest river in Europe, and the most important in Russia. Beyond the Ural Mountains, the Asian part of the USSR consists of the western Siberian lowlands, the mountainous area of central and eastern Siberia, the flat and partially desert area of central Asia reaching as far as the Pamirs, and the Far East, bounded by the Sea of Okhotsk and the Sea of Japan.

As may be expected from the extent of the country, there is a wide range of climate. In the tundra of the extreme north, the ground never really thaws out, whereas vines and tea plants grow in the south. Inland, the summers are hot and the winters extremely cold.

Once an agricultural country, the Soviet Union is now an industrial world power. Even the extensive collectivized agriculture is largely automated. The country is rich in mineral resources, the conditions for the exploitation of which in the eastern areas are being constantly improved. Scientifically and technically, the USSR is one of the leading nations of the world.

VATICAN CITY STATE *Area 0·17 sq mile (0·44 sq km); population 1,000; capital, Vatican City; currency, lira (Italian); official languages, Latin and Italian.*

The present-day frontiers of the Vatican, which lies wholly within Rome, were recognized by Italy in 1871, and the full and independent sovereignty of the Holy See was ratified in 1929. The museums of the Vatican are visited by hundreds of thousands of tourists every year.

YUGOSLAVIA *Area 98,750 sq miles (255,760 sq km); population, 21,500,000; capital, Belgrade (pop. 1,204,000); currency, dinar (100 paras); official languages, Serbo-Croatian, Slovene, and Macedonian.*

The present-day Socialist Federal Republic consists of six republics: Serbia, Slovenia, Croatia, Bosnia-Herzegovina, Montenegro, and Macedonia. Up to 1918, most of the country belonged to the Austro-Hungarian monarchy.

Bare karst mountains fringe the Adriatic Sea. Inland, most of the agriculturally exploitable plains lie along the Danube and its tributaries. The main crops are wheat, maize, tobacco, and vines, and stone fruits (plums, cherries) that are used in making highly popular alcoholic beverages. There are rich deposits of bauxite, lead, and zinc. The beautiful Adriatic coast has become an important centre of tourism.

ASIA

Asia, the largest of the continents, has an area of more than 17 million sq miles (44 million sq km). It is bigger than North America and South America put together. From its eastern frontier with Europe to its western shore on the Pacific Ocean it stretches for about 6,000 miles (9,600 km). In the north it has a coastline on the Arctic Ocean, but its southern limits are south of the equator.

Of all the continents, Asia has the greatest contrasts. In the mountain range of the Himalayas it has the world's highest peak, Mount Everest (29,028 ft; 8,848 m). The water-line of the Dead Sea, between Israel and Jordan, is the lowest point on the earth's surface, 1,286 ft (391 m) below sea-level. The exceptionally low temperature of −108·4°F (−78°C) has been recorded at the mouth of the River Lena in Siberia. But 132·8°F (56°C)—one of the highest climatic temperatures known—has been recorded in the Dasht-i-Lut, the Great Sandy Desert, in Iran. The contrast between summer and winter temperatures is nowhere greater than it is in central Asia. And the continent has other extreme weather conditions, too. At Cherrapunji in Assam, in north-eastern India, 1,041 inches (2,644 cm) of rain was measured in the course of 12 months.

More than half of all the people in the world live in Asia. The continent has many of the world's largest cities, including Tokyo (more than 11 million inhabitants), Shanghai (more than 10 million), and Peking (more than 7 million). About 40 other cities have several million inhabitants each. And yet vast areas of Asia are uninhabited, or very nearly so. Scarcely any people, for example, live on the steppes and deserts of the central regions, or on the tundra of the north. Nine-tenths of the continent's population is crowded together on the one-fifth of the land where it is possible to grow crops and build cities and other settlements. This contrast is best seen by comparing two countries such as Bangladesh and Mongolia. The former has a population density of 1,360 persons per square mile (525 per sq km), whereas the latter has a density of only a little over 2 persons per square mile (less than 1 per sq km).

Ever since prehistoric times, people have

THE FACE OF ASIA—A man and his oxen work slowly and patiently in a paddy-field

felt the compulsion to move from Asia's over-populated regions in search of better living conditions. Among the peoples of Asian descent who now live in other continents are the Eskimoes, who live in the Arctic parts of North America as well as in Asia, the American Indians, and the Europeans of Aryan-speaking ancestry. Some anthropologists believe that the ancestors of various Negro peoples in Africa may have emigrated to that continent from Asia. At a later stage of history, conquering Asian armies swept across the frontiers into Europe. They included Attila, the *Scourge of God,* and his Hun warriors in the AD 400s, and the armies of Genghis Khan in the 1200s and Tamerlane in the 1300s.

Asia is often called the *Cradle of Civilization* because it was in Asia that men began to develop the skills and ideas on which civilization was built. In the so-called *Fertile Crescent,* the valleys of the Tigris and Euphrates rivers in south-western Asia, people first turned from the hard, uncertain life of hunting and scavenging and learnt to cultivate the land and to raise animals for food. They may also have been the first to construct permanent houses and settlements. It was in Asia that men learnt to put copper, tin, and iron to use, that the art of writing was developed, and that alphabets were devised. Paper, gunpowder, and crop irrigation were among other Asian inventions and ideas. And, of course, it was in Asia that most of the world's major religions had their origin: Hinduism, Buddhism, Judaism, Christianity, Taoism, and Islam. Asian thinkers produced much of man's subtlest and most enduring philosophy.

TURKEY—The Hagia Sophia in Istanbul

SYRIA—Roman remains in the desert at Palmyra

INDIA—13th-century Kesava temple in Mysore
JAPAN—The Bull Arch in the Inland Sea at Miyajima

AFGHANISTAN *Area 250,000 sq miles (647,000 sq km); population 16,700,000; capital, Kabul (pop. 500,000); currency, afghani (100 puls); official languages, Dari Persian and Pushtu.*

The great mountain range of the HIndu Kush extends north-east to south-west across the country, some of its peaks rising to about 25,000 ft (7,600 m). The longest of the many rivers is the Helmand. Only some 4 per cent of the land is cultivated, and many people live as nomadic herdsmen, wandering over the mountain pastures with their herds of goats and karakul sheep. In the villages, cereals, sugar-beet, fruit, and cotton are grown. Exports include lambskins, carpets, and fruit. Manufactuhing industries are being developed.

BAHRAIN *Area 420 sq miles (1,080 sq km); population 216,000; capital, Manama (pop. 90,000); currency, dinar (1,000 fils); official language, Arabic.*

The state consists of several islands in the Persian Gulf, the largest of which is Bahrain Island. Once famous for its pearl fisheries, it has become rich by oil production. Its social services are highly developed.

BANGLADESH *Area 55,126 sq miles (142,776 sq km); population 75,000,000; capital, Dacca (pop. 1,700,000); currency, taka (100 paise); official languages, Bengali and Bihari.*

Until 1971, the country was East Pakistan, but in that year it broke away from Pakistan after a bloody civil war. Its territory consists of part of Assam and the old province of East Bengal. Much of it is an alluvial plain formed by the Ganges and the Jamuna. The delta of the Ganges, on the Bay of Bengal, is the world's largest. The chief products are jute, rice, tea, and tobacco.

BHUTAN *Area 18,000 sq miles (46,000 sq km); population 1,012,000; capital, Thimpu (pop. 8,000); currency, rupee (100 paise); official language, Dzongka.*

Small kingdom in the Himalayas, lying between Tibet (China) and India. Most of its people live in the fertile valleys in the centre of the country. The south has forested lowlands, and the north is fringed by high mountain peaks. The way of life is very similar to that of Tibet. Most of the people live by farming; their chief crops are rice, wheat, and barley.

BRUNEI *Area 2,226 sq miles (5,765 sq km); population 142,000; capital, Bandar Seri Begawan (pop. 38,000); currency, dollar (100 sen); languages, Malay, Chinese, and English.*

Brunei, on the northern coast of Borneo, is a self-governing sultanate. It is under British protection.

BURMA *Area 262,000 sq miles (679,000 sq km); population 29,512,000; capital, Rangoon (pop. 3,187,000); currency, kyat (100 pyas); official language, Burmese.*

The country became independent in 1948 after several generations of British rule. The Arakan Mountains extend along the western side of the country, and the eastern half is a high plateau, the Shan Massif. Between the mountains and the plateau is a lowland drained by the Irrawaddy and Sittang rivers. Another great river, the Salween, flows near the eastern border. A narrow strip of land, the Tenasserim Coast, stretches southwards to the Malay Peninsula. Burma is rich in mineral resources—oil, precious stones, and metals. The chief crops are rice, wheat, millet, sugarcane, ground-nuts, and tobacco. The forests yield teak and other woods. Most of the people are Burmans.

CHINA *Area 3,700,000 sq miles (9,600,000 sq km); population 800,500,000; capital, Peking (pop. 7,570,000); currency, yuan (10 chiao; 100 fen); official language, Chinese (Mandarin).*

The People's Republic of China, occupying more than one-fifth of Asia, is the home of about one-fifth of all the people in the world. Its history goes back nearly 4,000 years, and it has one of the oldest and most highly-developed civilizations. Vast areas of the country are almost uninhabited, but there are also many huge cities. In the east, there is a 4,250-mile (6,800-km) coastline on the Pacific Ocean. The Formosa Strait separates China from another Chinese country, Taiwan. On the south, west, and north, lofty mountain ranges form natural frontiers. The high plateau of Tibet in the south-west lies between the Kunlun Mountains (to the north) and the Himalayas, the world's highest mountain range (to the south). Beyond the Kunlun Mountains is the Takla Makan Desert. In the north, in Inner Mongolia, is part of another great desert, the Gobi.

The eastern part of China, the part where most of the people live, consists of two great river basins separated by the Chin Ling range. To the north of this range is the plain crossed by the Hwang Ho—the Yellow River, so called because of the yellow mud that colours its waters. To the south is the plain of the Yangtze-Kiang. These lowland regions are the historic China, the part of the country that the Great Wall was built to protect.

In the north and in the mountains the winters are bitterly cold. In the south, the climate is tropical or sub-tropical. The south-eastern coast suffers from typhoons and other destructive storms. In the interior, the rainfall is irregular and droughts and floods have caused famine from time immemorial. Today, dams and irrigation give some measure of protection. Rice and wheat are the chief crops. In the Yangtze valley as many as three rice crops are harvested each year. The government encourages the development of industry, but the economy is still mainly agricultural.

CYPRUS *Area 3,572 sq miles (9,251 sq km); population 633,000; capital, Nicosia (pop. 108,000); currency, pound (1,000 mils); official languages, Greek and Turkish.*

The island republic of Cyprus, in the Mediterranean Sea, was under British rule until 1960. Since independence it has suffered from conflict between the Greek majority (four-fifths of the population) and the Turkish minority. The island, the third largest in the Mediterranean, has two mountain ranges: the Kyrenia Range in the north, and the Troodos Mountains in the centre and west. Between these ranges lies a fertile plain, the Mesaoria. The country is rich in minerals, including copper and asbestos. Agriculturat products, such as cereals, wine, fruit, and tobacco, are the chief source of income.

HONG KONG *Area 398 sq miles (1,031 sq km); population 4,200,000; capital, Victoria (pop. 670,000); currency, dollar (100 cents); languages, English and Chinese.*

The British crown colony of Hong Kong, on the southern coast of China, consists of Hong Kong Island, more than 200 other small islands, and Kowloon and the New Territories on the mainland. It is an important financial, industrial, and trading centre.

INDIA *Area 1,262,000 sq miles (3,268,400 sq km); population 592,700,000; capital, New Delhi (pop. 4,070,000); currency, rupee (100 paise); official language, Hindi.*

Once 'the brightest jewel in the British crown', India has been independent since 1947. It has more people than any other country except China. India's civilization is one of the world's oldest, dating back to at least 2500 BC. The country occupies the greater part of the Indian Peninsula, its neighbours in the peninsula being Pakistan and Bangladesh. Its coastline on the Indian Ocean measures some 4,250 miles (6,800 km). The terrain is very varied. Foothills of the Himalayas extend along 1,500 miles (2,400 km) of the northern border. To their south, the alluvial lowlands of the Northern Plains stretch right across the widest part of the peninsula. They have India's richest farming land, and are heavily populated. Still farther south is the Deccan Plateau, occupying the greater part of the peninsula. On both coastal edges it rises to mountain ranges called the *Ghats*. Almost all parts of the country are crossed by great rivers, but the most important are in the north: the Indus, the Ganges, and the Brahmaputra. In most areas, the south-west monsoon brings heavy rains each year from June to September. Much of the country is very hot, the coolest areas being in the hills and on the west coast. Rice and wheat are the most important crops. Other crops are millet, ground-nuts, bananas, cotton, rapeseed, linseed, and jute. There are great numbers of cattle, sheep, and goats; cattle are sacred to the Hindus and are not used for food. The most important manufactures are textiles, but the development of other industries is a major part of government planning. One of the country's most serious problems is over-population.

INDONESIA *Area 735,000 sq miles (1,904,000 sq km); population 128,000,000; capital, Djakarta (pop. 5,000,000); currency, rupiah (100 sen); official language, Bahasa Indonesian.*

The country consists of about 3,000 islands grouped between the Indian and Pacific oceans. The largest are Sumatra, Celebes, and Java. Indonesia shares two other large islands: Borneo with Malaysia, and New Guinea with Papua New Guinea. Most of the larger islands are mountainous and volcanic. There are more than 200 volcanoes, of which about 60 are active and 125 more eject sulphur fumes. The most densely populated island is Java: more than half of all Indonesians live on it and it is the seat of the government. It has rich agricultural land in the north, and it is well known for its wax-printed fabric, called *batik*. Many of the other, lightly-populated islands are thickly forested, and some are swampy. The climate is generally humid and sultry, the hottest regions being on the islands that lie on the equator —Sumatra and Kalimantan (the Indonesian part of Borneo), for example. All the islands are affected by the monsoons. Indonesia has rich mineral deposits, chiefly petroleum, tin, and bauxite. Rubber, tea, coffee, tobacco, and sugar are grown on plantations. The chief subsistence crops are rice and other cereals, bananas, spices, and beans.

The ancient and beautiful city of Esfahan stands near an oasis on the great central plateau of Iran. Under Shah Abbas I, Esfahan was again the capital of an empire. Among the magnificent buildings begun during his reign was the imperial mosque (*right*), the foundations of which were laid in 1612. One of the masterpieces of Islamic art, it is crowned by a turquoise-coloured dome of majolica. The mosaics depict branches, interspersed with quotations from the Koran.

IRAN *Area 680,000 sq miles (1,626,500 sq km); population 31,000,000; capital Tehran (pop. 3,200,000); currency, rial (100 dinars); official language, Farsi (Persian).*

The kingdom of Iran lies between the Caspian Sea in the north, and the Persian Gulf and Arabian Sea in the south. It is often called *Persia*. It is mostly a vast, mountain-fringed plateau, averaging some 4,000 ft (1,200 m) above sea-level. However, part of the Great Sand Desert, the Dasht-i-Lut, in the east-centre is some 800 ft (250 m) below sea-level. This desert is one of the hottest in the world. To its north is the Great Salt Desert, the Dasht-i-Kavir. The northern coastal strip is the only major agricultural area, and the chief crops are cereals, tea, fruit, and cotton. Several million people live nomadic lives as herdsmen. The rich mineral deposits include petroleum.

IRAQ *Area 172,000 sq miles (445,500 sq km); population 10,200,000; capital, Baghdad (pop. 700,000); currency, dinar (1,000 fils); official language, Arabic.*

The country has been independent since 1958; previously it had been under Turkish and, from 1920, British rule. The lowlands in the centre of Iraq are the basins of the Tigris and Euphrates rivers. These great rivers are the frontiers of the historic region of *Mesopotamia*, 'the country between the rivers'. On the north, the lowlands are bordered

Right: A Bedouin in Kuwait holds a falcon on his gloved hand. The art of falconry—using trained birds of prey for hunting—originated in Asia.

Below: Laying an oil pipeline in Syria. Oil is the main source of revenue—often the only important source—in many countries of the Middle East.

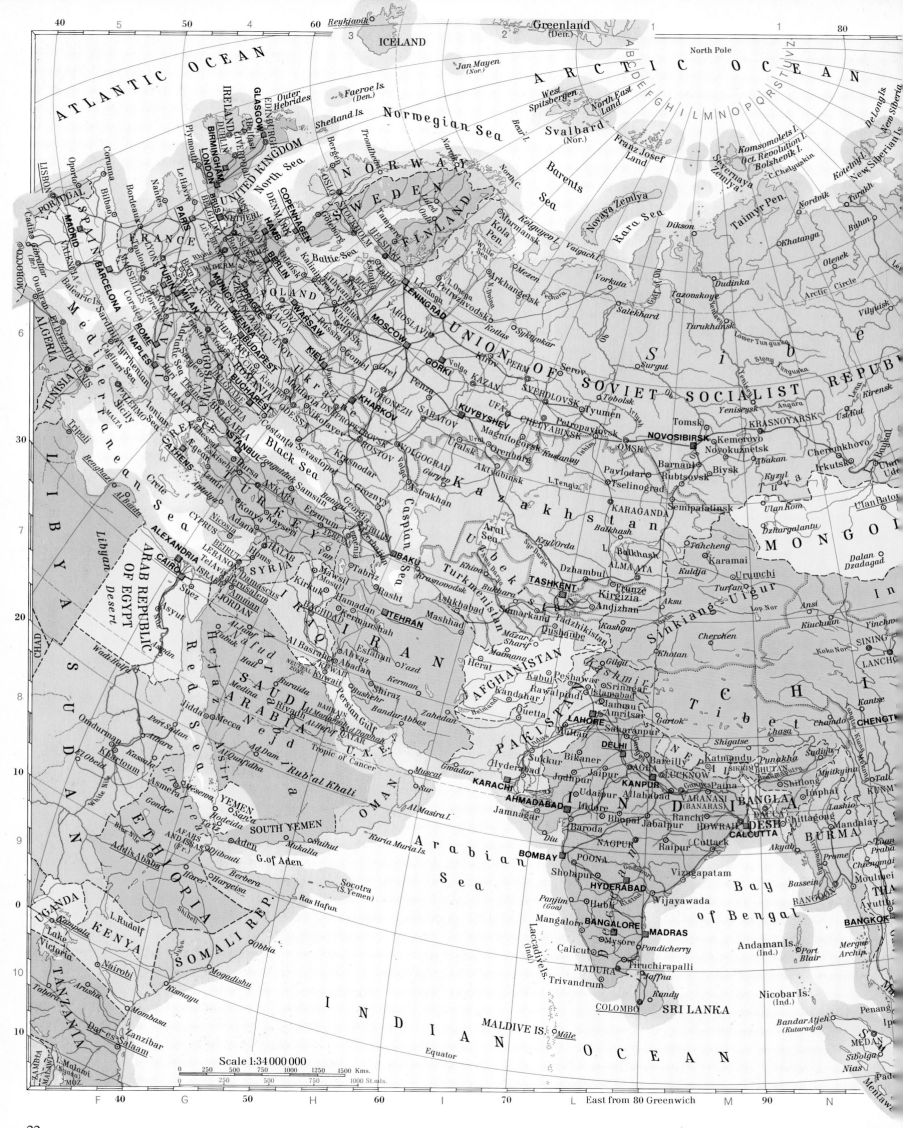

Ocean, separated from the Asian mainland by the Sea of Japan. There are four main islands: Honshu, Hokkaido, Kyushu, and Shikoku. Among the more than 3,000 smaller islands there are two major groups: the Ryukyus and the Bonins. Most of the islands are mountainous, the highest peaks being on Honshu. Among them is Fujiyama, the highest mountain in Japan, which rises to 12,388 ft (3,776 m). This snow-mantled peak is a volcano, but not active. There are nearly 200 other volcanoes, some of which erupt from time to time. Earthquakes are frequent, but generally they cause only minor damage. The islands have many rivers, some of which are very fast-flowing, and are consequently suitable for the production of hydro-electricity. Most of Japan's farms are small. The chief crops are rice and other cereals, fruit, and vegetables. But because only a small part of the land can be cultivated, Japan has to import much of its food. It also has to import most of the raw materials that feed its industries. In spite of this, the country has raised itself to the front rank of industrial powers, and has a leading place among producers of optical goods, cameras, radio and television equipment, and motor vehicles, including motor-cycles. It is also a major shipbuilding country, and it has built up one of the world's largest fishing fleets. Japan is very densely populated but—in contrast to most other Asian countries—its population has risen slowly in recent years.

Mount Everest (29,028 ft; 8,848 m), the highest mountain in the world, is in the Himalaya range, on the border between Nepal and Tibet. It is named after Sir George Everest, who was surveyor-general of India in the 1830s. The Nepalese call it *Sagarmatha*, and the Tibetans *Chono-Lungma*. For many years, the seemingly unclimbable mountain tempted and challenged climbers, until eventually, in 1953, an expedition—the eighth to make the attempt —reached its summit.

Below: The Hindu temple of Chindambaram, in India, richly decorated with thousands of pieces of sculpture. Hinduism, the chief religion of India, has more than 400 million followers. They believe in Brahman, the supreme spirit, who is beyond man's full understanding. The supreme spirit is worshipped in three forms: Brahma, who creates the world; Vishnu, who preserves it; and Siva, who destroys it.

by wooded hills, which are part of *Kurdistan*. The people of this region, the Kurds, look upon themselves as a separate nation. In the west of Iraq are the barren wastes of the Syrian Desert. The country's chief source of revenue is petroleum, and it has other minerals, too. Cereals, cotton, vegetables, and tobacco are the principal agricultural products.

ISRAEL *Area 7,992 sq miles (20,700 sq km); population 3,200,000; capital, Jerusalem (pop. 300,000); currency, pound (100 agorot); official languages, Hebrew and Arabic.*

Since its foundation in 1948, Israel has fought several small wars against hostile Arab neighbours. About half of the country is occupied by the Negev Desert, but the north is mountainous and there is also a low-lying coastal strip. Much desert land has been made arable by being cleared and irrigated. This pioneer work was carried out by *kibbutzim*, community settlements. Intensive agriculture is of major importance to the economy. The chief products are cereals, citrus fruits, grapes (for eating and for wine), and vegetables. There are textile, engineering, and chemical industries in addition to food processing. Israel's mineral resources include potash, phosphates, oil, and natural gas.

JAPAN *Area 142,810 sq miles (369,880 sq km); population 106,800,000; capital Tokyo (pop. 11,600,000); currency, yen; official language, Japanese.*

Nippon Koku, 'the Land of the Rising Sun', has an emperor who belongs to one of the world's oldest ruling dynasties. The country consists of an archipelago in the Pacific

JORDAN *Area 37,700 sq miles (97,600 sq km); population 2,600,000; capital, Amman (pop. 584,000); currency, dinar (1,000 fils); official language, Arabic.*

The Hashemite Kingdom of the Jordan is a mountainous country lying mainly to the east of the Jordan River. At the southern end of the river is the Dead Sea, the earth's lowest surface point. The north-east of the country is part of the barren Syrian Desert. Only one-tenth of the land is agriculturally productive. The chief crops are cereals, olives, citrus fruits, and tomatoes. Phosphates and some other minerals are exported, and there are some manufacturing industries and oil refining.

Right: Decorated elephants in a religious procession in Nepal. The Nepalese kingdom is in the great mountain range of the Himalayas. Most Nepalese are Gurkhas, but there are other national groups, too, such as the Sherpas. The state religion is Hinduism. There are also some Buddhists, many of them living near the frontier with Tibet.

KHMER REPUBLIC *Area 70,000 sq miles (181,000 sq km); population 7,200,000; capital, Phnom Penh (pop. 2,000,000); currency, riel (100 sen); official language, Khmer.*

The Khmer Republic in Indochina was formerly the kingdom of Cambodia. Much of the country lies in the fertile alluvial basin of the Mekong River, but there are mountains in the north and south-west. Most people live by farming or fishing. The chief subsistence crop is rice, and other crops include cotton, pepper, tobacco, and rubber. Fish are taken from the Tonle Sap, the 'Great Lake', in the west.

KOREA, NORTH *Area 46,800 sq miles (121,200 sq km); population 15,000,000; capital, Pyongyang (pop. 1,500,000); currency, won (100 jun); official language, Korean.*

The peninsula of Korea on the north-east coast of China is separated from Japan by the Korea Strait. In 1910 it was annexed by Japan, and after World War II was occupied by Russian troops (in the north) and American troops (in the south). In 1948, the two occupation zones became separate states. A conflict between the two states from 1950 to 1953 involved several other countries, too, including the United States, China, Britain, and France. It ended with agreement that the 38° parallel should form the boundary between the two Koreas. North Korea, the Democratic People's Republic of Korea, is mountainous and is very rich in minerals. It also has textile and engineering industries. The small amount of arable land is productive, the chief crops being cereals and cotton.

KOREA, SOUTH *Area 38,400 sq miles (99,460 sq km); population 34,000,000; capital Seoul (pop. 5,600,000); currency, won (100 jun); official language, Korean.*

The Republic of Korea occupies the southern part of the Korean Peninsula. It is generally mountainous, but the valleys and the southern plains are fertile. The chief crops are rice, vegetables, fruit, soya beans, and groundnuts. Manufactures include electrical goods and textiles, and there are some exports of minerals.

KUWAIT *Area 7,500 sq miles (19,000 sq km); population 900,000; capital, Kuwait City (pop. 300,000); currency, dinar (1,000 fils); official language, Arabic.*

The small, desert country of Kuwait has one of the world's highest *per capita* incomes as a result of its production of petroleum. It is believed to have about one-fifth of the world's known oil resources. It also produces natural gas. Much of its labour force consists of foreign workers from Saudi Arabia, Egypt, and other countries. There are highly-developed social services.

LAOS *Area 91,400 sq miles (236,725 sq km); population 3,100,000; capital, Vientiane (pop. 174,000); currency, kip; official language, Lao.*

Laos, fully independent since 1954, was formerly part of French Indochina. The country is landlocked, and its northern part is mountainous and heavily forested. In the south the land descends to the Mekong River; this region is relatively fertile. The chief subsistence crops are rice and other cereals, but coffee, cotton, tea, and tobacco are also grown. The most important export is tin. Teak and other woods are exported, too.

Above: Workers on a community farm near Peking, in China. China is in the process of trying to turn itself into an industrial power, but it still remains predominantly an agricultural country. The most important crop is rice, which is the main item of the people's diet. Other cereals are grown, too, as well as soya beans, tea, and cotton. Improved methods of irrigation and terracing have made it possible to bring more land into cultivation. Dams are built to protect the land against flooding when the rivers swell. Mechanization of farm work is still in its early stages, and in many regions the bulk of the work is carried out slowly and laboriously by hand. All land is owned collectively, and farm produce is shared out. Village communes have their own shops; they keep few luxuries, but their stock is often large and varied.

Centre: A Mongolian herdsman on the great, open plateaux. It is often said that Mongolia has two horses for each member of its population. The country is the home of bold and skilful horsemen. Centuries ago, their ancestors ventured as far as Europe, and, under Genghis Khan, established a powerful kingdom.

A new road through the taiga in Siberia. The taiga, the vast belt of coniferous forest that stretches across northern Europe and Asia, includes more than a quarter of all the forest land in the world. Much of it is almost uninhabited.

25

The Emerald Temple in the colourful and romantic city of Bangkok, in Thailand. The temple stands in an inner courtyard of the Grand Palace—the small, walled, 18th-century royal city. The gigantic statues of guardian deities watch over those who enter the sanctuary. Inside, a golden Buddha lies on a gilded throne. Buddhism is the religion of most of the people of the Indochina Peninsula. It originated in India, but has found most of its adherents and its deepest expression in other countries.

LEBANON *Area 4,300 sq miles (11,000 sq km); population 2,700,000; capital, Beirut (pop. 600,000); currency, pound (100 piastres); official language, Arabic.*

Lebanon became an independent country in 1946. Earlier, it had been part of the Ottoman Empire and, after World War I, a French mandated territory. It has a narrow coastal strip on the eastern Mediterranean, behind which rise the Lebanon Mountains. Farther inland is the Fertile Bekaa Valley, and then the heights of the Anti-Lebanon Mountains along the frontier with Syria. Only about one-third of the land is suitable for agriculture, the chief crops being citrus fruits, apples, grapes, olives, bananas, and tobacco. The country has many industries, and is an important financial and commercial centre. It is the only Arab state in which the Christian population is influential.

MACAO *Area 5 sq miles (8 sq km); population 320,000; capital, Macao (pop. 320,000); currency, pataca (100 avos); languages, Portuguese and Cantonese.*

Macao is an overseas province of Portugal. It consists of two small islands and a mainland peninsula at the mouth of the Canton River in southern China. It is a popular tourist centre.

MALAYSIA *Area 130,000 sq miles (337,000 sq km); population 11,800,000; capital, Kuala Lumpur (pop. 770,000); currency, dollar (100 cents); official language, Malay.*

The Federation of Malaysia became an independent country in 1963. Its territory consists of former British-ruled states in the southern part of the Malay Peninsula and the northern part of the island of Borneo. The peninsular regions are called *West Malaysia,* and those in Borneo *East Malaysia.* West Malaysia is separated by the Johore Strait from Singapore, which was part of the Federation until 1965. The peninsula has a mountain backbone; the western coastal plain is considerably wider than that in the east. East Malaysia is extremely mountainous, its high-

The British colony of Hong Kong, in south-east China, lies near the mouth of the Pearl River. It has one of the most important ports in the world, and is one of Asia's chief centres of commerce, providing China with a ready outlet for its goods. The pressure of population in Hong Kong brings many problems. *Left:* More than 100,000 people live on boats called sampans. *Right:* In the crowded streets, rickshaws cause fewer traffic jams than taxis.

est peak, Mount Kinabalu, rising to 13,450 ft (4,100 m). About two-thirds of Malaysia is covered by thick rain forest. Rubber and timber are among the valuable forest products; Malaysia is one of the two leading rubber producers in the world. There are rich deposits of tin, as well as mineral oils, iron, and bauxite. On the lowlands rice, peppers, and pineapples are grown.

MALDIVES
Area 115 sq miles (298 sq km); population 114,000; capital, Malé (pop. 14,000); currency, rupee; official language, Maldivian.

The Maldives, a former British protectorate, consist of a chain of 12 atolls about 400 miles (640 km) south-west of Sri Lanka in the Indian Ocean. Altogether, there are about 2,000 coral islands of which some 200 are inhabited. No point is more than 8 ft (2·4 m) above sea-level.

MONGOLIA
Area 600,000 sq miles (1,550,000 sq km); population 1,400,000; capital Ulan Bator (pop. 250,000); currency, tugrik (100 möngö); official language, Khalkha Mongolian.

From the 1600s to 1912, Mongolia was a Chinese province; its status was then in doubt until 1946 when China recognized its independence. It is now called the *Mongolian People's Republic.* Most of it consists of vast plateaux ringed by chains of mountains in the north and east. In the south-east is part of the Gobi Desert. Many of the people are herdsmen, but in recent years efforts have been made to develop agriculture. The country's mineral resources include coal, oil, and non-ferrous metals.

NEPAL
Area 54,362 sq miles (140,797 sq km); population 11,600,000; capital, Katmandu (pop. 354,000); currency, rupee (100 pice); official language, Nepali.

The Hindu kingdom of Nepal lies on the southern flank of the Himalayas, and Mount Everest (29,028 ft; 8,848 m) towers above its northern frontier. Most of the country is mountainous, and it has also thick jungles and swamps. The chief crops are rice and other cereals, and jute. In the villages, textiles and other woven goods are produced.

OMAN
Area 82,000 sq miles (212,000 sq km); population 690,000; capital, Muscat (pop. 7,000); currency, rial Omani (1,000 baiza); official language, Arabic.

The sultanate of Oman, in the south-east of the Arabian Peninsula, has a long coastline on the Arabian Sea. The centre is low-lying but barren. In the north-east there are hills, and in the south-west the hot Dhofar Plateau. The chief exports are oil, dates, fish, and pearls.

PAKISTAN
Area 310,400 sq miles (804,000 sq km); population 64,800,000; capital, Islamabad (pop. 235,000); currency, rupee (100 paisas); official language, Urdu.

Until 1947, the land that is now Pakistan was part of the British-ruled Indian Empire. In 1971, part of Pakistan—separated from the rest of the country by 900 miles (1,500 km) of Indian territory—broke away and formed the independent nation of Bangladesh after a bloody civil war. Great mountain ranges rise along the north and north-west frontiers—the Himalaya, Hindu Kush, and Karakoram systems. On the boundary with Afghanistan is the Khyber Pass. About one-third of the country is a great plain, watered by the Indus. This

plain was the site of one of the earliest civilizations. The climate is strongly affected by the monsoons. Much of the country's agriculture depends on artificial irrigation. Cotton and rice are exported. There are textile, chemical, and other industries.

PHILIPPINES
Area 115,800 sq miles (299,900 sq km); population 42,600,000; capital, Quezon City (pop. 590,000); currency, peso (100 centavos); official language, Pilipino.

The Philippines has been independent since 1946. Before that, it was ruled by Spain for 300 years, and, after 1898, by the United States. The country consists of more than 7,000 islands, extending for some 1,000 miles (1,600 km) between the Pacific Ocean and the South China Sea. The three largest islands are Luzon, Mindanao, and Palawan. About 700 islands are inhabited. Most of the islands are mountainous, and some have volcanoes. The chief crops are cereals, fruits, sugar, sweet potatoes, and hemp. There are valuable mineral deposits.

QATAR
Area 4,000 sq miles (10,300 sq km); population 150,000; capital, Doha (pop. 90,000); currency, riyal (100 dirhams); official language, Arabic.

The sheikdom of Qatar occupies a 120-mile (190-km) long peninsula jutting northwards from the coast of Saudi Arabia into the Persian Gulf. Once a land of nomadic herdsmen, fishermen, and pearl divers, it has become a rich and important oil producing state.

SAUDI ARABIA
Area 920,000 sq miles (2,383,000 sq km); population 8,300,000; capital, Riyadh (pop. 450,000); currency, riyal (20 qursh); official language, Arabic.

The kingdom of Saudi Arabia occupies the greater part of the Arabian Peninsula. The mountains of the Hejaz and Asir ranges extend along the west coast. Inland are rocky plateaux and deserts, the largest deserts being the An Nafud in the north, and the Rub'al Khali, the Empty Quarter, in the south.

A paddy field in the Khmer Republic. This method of rice cultivation has been used for perhaps as long as 5,000 years. It provides rich harvests. The first of man's agricultural techniques were developed in Asia, and in many places the soil is still tilled today as it was in the distant past. In most of Asia, agriculture is of far greater importance than industry, commerce, or any other occupation. A Chinese proverb says: 'Man can live without a roof or walls, but not without a daily bowl of rice.'

Women in Vietnam. One of them is grinding grain with a hand mill.

A Malaysian village in Sarawak, on the island of Borneo. The two parts of the Federation of Malaysia—the southern region of the Malay Peninsula, and the northern region of Borneo—are separated by 1,000 miles (1,600 km) of the South China Sea. There are a few major towns, but most of the people live in small villages. Many work on rubber plantations; Malaysia is a leading producer of rubber.

A temple dancer of Bali, in Indonesia. Bali, one of the Lesser Sunda Islands, lies between the Java Sea and the Indian Ocean, and has many volcanoes. It is famous for its beautiful scenery.

There are no permanent rivers. Many nomads roam the sandy wastes. The country has enormous revenues from oil production.

SINGAPORE   *Area 224 sq miles (580 sq km); population 2,200,000; capital, Singapore (pop. 1,240,000); currency, dollar (100 cents); official languages, Malay, Mandarin, Tamil, and English.*

The island country of Singapore is separated from the southern tip of the Malay Peninsula by the narrow Johore Strait. Until 1965 it was part of Malaysia, and before that was a British crown colony. Most of the island is low-lying. It owes its importance to its fine harbour and its usefulness as a trade centre. In recent years it has greatly developed its industries. Its population is predominantly Chinese. The next largest group is Malay.

SRI LANKA   *Area 25,332 sq miles (65,610 sq km); population 12,748,000; capital, Colombo (pop. 565,000); currency, rupee (100 cents); official language, Sinhala.*

Island country in the Indian Ocean, off the southern tip of India. It was formerly called *Ceylon* and was British-ruled until 1948. Most of the island is a fertile plain, but the southern part has mountains that rise to 8,400 ft (2,550 m). Rice, tea, palms, and fruit grow in the tropical monsoon climate, and the forests provide rubber and valuable woods. Most of the people are Sinhalese, but there is a large Tamil minority. Unlike the Buddhist Sinhalese, the Tamils—who emigrated to Sri Lanka from southern India—are Hindus.

SYRIA   *Area 71,800 sq miles (185,960 sq km); population 6,600,000; capital, Damascus (pop. 560,000); currency, pound (100 piastres); official language, Arabic.*

Syria became independent in 1946. Before that it had been ruled as a mandated territory by the French, and, until 1919, as part of the Ottoman Empire. The south of the country is in the Syrian Desert, to the north of which is the broad and fertile valley of the River Euphrates. The chief crops are cereals, cotton, fruit, and tobacco. Oil pipelines cross the desert to Mediterranean ports.

TAIWAN   *Area 13,885 sq miles (35,962 sq km); population 15,200,000; capital, Taipei (pop. 1,920,000); currency, dollar (100 cents); official language, Chinese (Mandarin).*

The island of Taiwan, or Formosa, in the Pacific Ocean is separated from the Chinese mainland by the Formosa Strait. In 1895, it was ceded to Japan by treaty, but it was returned to China in 1945 after World War II. In 1949, Chiang Kai-shek withdrew to Taiwan after the civil war in which he and his supporters were defeated by the communists. He established a Chinese Nationalist republic with the military protection of the United States. Two-thirds of the island is mountainous. The inhabitants live mainly on the fertile western coastal plain. The chief crops are rice, sugar, fruit, and vegetables. Fishing is important, and there are many manufacturing industries.

THAILAND   *Area 198,460 sq miles (513,810 sq km); population 36,000,000; capital, Bangkok (pop. 2,500,000); currency, baht (100 satangs); official language, Thai.*

Thailand was for long known as *Siam*. The northern part of the country is on the Asian mainland, but a southern 'tail' stretches into the Malay Peninsula. In the far north, between the Mekong and Salween rivers, Thailand is mountainous. In the east is a high tableland. The centre heartland is the vast, fertile floodplain of the Chao Phraya (Menam) River. Rain and monsoon forests cover two-thirds of the country, and there are mangrove swamps along the wet southern coast. The most important crop is rice, the yield of which has been greatly increased by irrigation works. Rubber is the chief cash crop. Fishing is a major source of food. The country's natural resources include valuable woods, such as teak, from the forests, and tin, tungsten, and other minerals. There are almost no roads; river and canal transport is widely used.

TIMOR, PORTUGUESE   *Area 7,330 sq miles (19,000 sq km); population 620,000; capital, Dili (pop. 11,000).*

Portuguese Timor consists of the eastern part of Timor Island in the Malay Archipelago, and a few other tiny territories. The western part of Timor belongs to Indonesia. Rice, sweet potatoes, coffee, and rubber are produced.

TURKEY   *Area 301,300 sq miles (780,360 sq km); population 37,600,000; capital, Ankara (pop. 1,480,000); currency, lira (100 kurus); official language, Turkish.*

Formerly the centre of the Ottoman Empire, Turkey became a republic in 1923. The greater part of the country is in Asia, but a small part is in Europe, across the Dardanelles, the Sea of Marmara, and the Bosporus. European Turkey is mainly low-lying, but the vast, broken Anatolian Plateau occupies much of the Asian section. To the north of the plateau are the Pontine Mountains, and to the south the Taurus Mountains. On the coasts and in the Taurus valleys the climate is mild. Crops include fruit, cereals, cotton, and tobacco. In the rugged highlands there are large flocks of sheep. Textiles and iron and steel are manufactured.

UNITED ARAB EMIRATES   *Area 32,000 sq miles (82,000 sq km); population 300,000; capital Abu Dhabi (pop. 60,000); currency, dirham (100 fils); official language, Arabic.*

The U.A.E. is a federation of seven sheikhdoms or emirates on the Persian Gulf, formerly known as the *Trucial States*: Abu Dhabi, Dubai, Sharjah, Ajman, Umm al Qaiwain, Ras al Khaimah, and Fujairah. The land is mostly desert, but there are rich oilfields in Abu Dhabi and elsewhere.

Fujiyama or Fujisan, on the island of Honshu, about 70 miles (112 km) from Tokyo, is Japan's highest mountain. For many Japanese, it is sacred, and it rises isolated and magnificent above its surroundings. The plain around Fujiyama is intensively cultivated.

VIETNAM Area 128,400 sq miles (332,560 sq km); population 42,300,000; chief cities, (north) Hanoi (pop. 920,000), (south) Saigon or Ho Chi Minh City (pop. 1,700,000); currency, dong (100 xu); official language, Vietnamese.

Formerly part of French Indochina, Vietnam was divided from 1954 to 1975 into a communist state in the north and a non-communist state in the south. Then, a protracted and bloody war ended in a communist victory. The country is about 1,000 miles (1,600 km) long, but is less than 50 miles (80 km) across at its narrowest point. The centre of Vietnam is a fertile coastal plain. In the north is the delta of the Red River, and in the south the delta of the Mekong River. There are many forests and marshes. The chief crop is rice, and other crops are coffee, tea, sugar, tobacco, and sweet potatoes. Rubber, quinine, and cinnamon are exported.

YEMEN (Aden) Area 180,000 sqiles (466,000 sq km); population 1,600,000; capital, Aden (pop. 250,000); currency, dinar (1,000 fils); official language, Arabic.

The People's Democratic Republic of Yemen was formerly under British rule, and became independent in 1967. It is on the south-west coast of the Arabian Peninsula. Its sandy coastal plain is separated from the interior desert by highlands. Many of the people are nomadic herdsmen, and fishing is important. Cotton, coffee, and skins are exported.

YEMEN (San'a) Area 75,000 sq miles (194,000 sq km); population 6,000,000; capital, San'a (pop. 120,000); currency, riyal (40 bogaches); official language, Arabic.

The Yemen Arab Republic has a broad, sandy coastal strip along the Red Sea; this gives way to highlands, which occupy most of the interior of the country. Coastal areas have little rain, and are unproductive agriculturally. But the highlands have higher rainfall and have many fertile river valleys. Most of the people are herdsmen or subsistence farmers. Coffee, skins, and gum arabic are exported. The only important mineral product is salt.

The Temple of Dai-goji in the old Japanese city of Kyoto, at cherry-blossom time. Japan is a land of small gardens and groves that, by long-standing tradition, are cared for lovingly. The blossoming of the cherry is considered a special event of the year, and many people go on outings to the country to celebrate the coming of spring.

AFRICA

THE UNTAMED BEAUTY OF AFRICA—A herd of elephants in Tanzania. In the background, the snow-capped summit of Kilimanjaro, the continent's highest mountain.

In the Middle Ages little was known of Africa south of the Sahara. Scholars were familiar with the great ancient civilizations of the north, and many European travellers had visited the lands just across the Mediterranean Sea. The Moors from northern Africa had even established kingdoms in Europe. But practically nothing had been discovered of Negro Africa—of the Mandingo Empire, for example, or of the Songhai Empire. Most of the African continent was still hidden and a mystery. However, by the 1500s European navigators were aware that the continent was enormous, because in the 1490s Vasco da Gama had sailed round the Cape to India. In the same century, European trading settlements were established along the African coasts. And Europeans, Arabs, and Negroes par-

ticipated in the terrible trade in slaves. Over the years, some 15 million Africans were sold into slavery, chiefly in the Americas.

In the 18th century, explorers from Europe began to penetrate into the interior of Africa. The upper course of the Nile was explored, and the Sahara was crossed. In the 1800s, David Livingstone's reports of his discoveries during journeys across the continent created a sensation. The natural wealth of Africa attracted the interest of commercial companies and also of their governments. In the second half of the 19th century, a race began to carve up the continent. The king of the Belgians acquired a huge tract of territory in the basin of the Congo River as his personal property. Britain, France, Spain, Portugal,

the Netherlands, and Germany extended their possessions and influence in Africa.

The conquest of Africa was relatively easy for the countries of Europe. Most Africans lived in loosely-knit tribal groups. Few tribes felt any strong communal interests with any other tribes, and it was difficult for such leaders as arose to organize resistance to the invaders.

Most of the people of Africa are Negroes, a term derived from the Latin word *niger*, meaning *black*. Anthropologists do not know their origin, but it seems certain that they were not the continent's original inhabitants. They may have migrated to Africa from Asia in prehistoric times. There is some evidence that they may have settled first in an area to the south of the Sahara and then, later, spread to other regions.

In the course of time, three main ethnic groups developed among the Negroes: the Sudanese in the northern regions; the Nilotes along the upper Nile and in Kenya; and the Bantu in the equatorial belt and the south. There are also smaller groups, such as the Bushmen, the Negrillos (pygmies), and the Hottentots. The languages and dialects of these Negroid peoples are extremely varied.

The non-Negroid peoples of northern and eastern Africa are mostly of Semitic or Hamitic origin. The Semites are mainly Arabs. The Hamites include the Egyptians, Ethiopians, Berbers, and Somalis, as well as some Arabs. In northern Africa, most people speak Arabic. In the east, Swahili has become a commercial lingua franca used in addition to tribal or other national languages.

In the years following World War II, a tremendous 'silent revolution' took place in Africa as European countries gave up their colonies one by one, and new, independent African countries took shape. Some of them have retained close ties with the former colonial powers. Often, the colonial languages—principally English and French—have been freely retained. Many of the leaders of the new Africa subscribe to the idea of pan-Africanism, the aim of which is the eventual union of all the African peoples.

AFARS AND ISSAS, TERRITORY OF THE
Area 9,000 sq miles (23,300 sq km); population 101,000; capital, Djibouti (pop. 62,000); official language, French.

Formerly known as *French Somaliland*, the territory was renamed in 1967 and granted its independence in 1976. It is an arid, hilly, desert land, but swampy in coastal districts. Farming is at a subsistence level, heavily dependent on livestock.

ALGERIA
Area 918,000 sq miles (2,378,000 sq km); population 15,200,000; capital, Algiers (El Djezair; pop. 1,100,000); currency, dinar (100 centimes); official language, Arabic.

Algeria has been an independent country since 1962. In that year, the French government, which had ruled Algeria for more than one hundred years, relinquished control. Nine-tenths of the country is in the Sahara, and is inhabited only around oases or by nomads. But the coastal strip between the Mediterranean Sea and the northern flank of the Atlas Mountains is fertile and thickly populated. Most of the towns are in this region, which has rich crops of cereals, vegetables, and early fruits. Wine is important, too. Algeria has valuable deposits of petroleum, natural gas, and phosphates.

ANGOLA
Area 481,350 sq miles (1,246,700 sq km); population 5,700,000; capital, Luanda (pop. 347,000); currency, escudo (100 centavos); official languages, Portuguese and Bantu.

Until 1975, Angola was a Portuguese colony. Apart from a long coastal plain, the country consists mainly of the vast Bié Plateau. Important crops include coffee, sugar-cane, cotton, and oil palms, and there are deposits of oil, iron, and other minerals.

BOTSWANA
Area 220,000 sq miles (570,000 sq km); population 650,000; capital, Gaborones (pop. 18,000); currency, rand (100 cents); official language, English.

The republic of Botswana, which became independent in 1966, was formerly the British protectorate of Bechuanaland. The country is a plateau, the southern part of which is occupied by the Kalahari Desert, an arid region of thorn savanna. In the desert, only Bushmen and small groups of Bantu live. The huge, swampy Okovanggo Basin in the north is formed by the Okovanggo River. Cereals, pulses, and cotton are grown.

BURUNDI
Area 10,747 sq miles (27,835 sq km); population 3,700,000; capital, Bujumbura (pop. 70,000); currency, franc; official languages, French and Kirundi.

Burundi lies on the north-eastern bank of Lake Tanganyika. It was once a German colony, and later a Belgian mandated territory. Most of the country lies on a plateau, but there are mountains in the west; these mark the edge of the African Rift Valley, in which Lake Tanganyika lies. The savanna highlands have good pastures. Rice and other cereals are grown, as well as coffee and cotton.

CAMEROON
Area 183,570 sq miles (475,444 sq km); population 6,100,000; capital, Yaoundé (pop. 180,000); currency, franc; official languages, French and English.

The Federal Republic of Cameroon was fohmed in 1961 from French and British trust territories that had previously been part of the German colony of Kamerun. The coastal plain on the Gulf of Guinea is marshy, and slopes upwards to the mountainous plateau that occupies most of the country. In the centre, the Adamawa Highlands rise to some 6,000 ft (1,800 m). Half the country is thickly forested. Palm oil, rubber, and timber are important to the economy. The chief crops are cocoa and coffee.

CANARY ISLANDS
Area 2,807 sq miles (7,270 sq km); population 1,165,000; capital, Las Palmas (on Gran Canaria; pop. 287,000); currency, peseta; official language, Spanish.

Group of islands some 60 miles (97 km) off the north-west coast of Africa, making up two provinces of Spain. There are six tiny islands and seven large ones, including Tenerife.

CENTRAL AFRICAN REPUBLIC
Area 234,000 sq miles (606,000 sq km); population 1,800,000; capital, Bangui (pop. 300,000); currency, franc; official languages, French and Sango.

The republic was a French colony before independence in 1960. It lies in the centre of the continent. It is mainly a hilly plateau, forested in the south. The chief rivers are the Ubangi and the Bomu. Cotton, coffee, and ground-nuts are exported. There are some minerals, including gold and industrial diamonds.

CHAD
Area 495,750 sq miles (1,284,000 sq km); population 4,000,000; capital, N'djaména (Fort Lamy; pop. 126,000); currency, franc; official language, French.

Chad, a former French colony, became independent in 1960. It is named after Lake Chad, on its western border. The northern part of the country, in the Sahara, includes the high Tibesti Mountains. The south is savanna, some of it plateau country. Cotton and ground-nuts are exported.

CONGO
Area 129,000 sq miles (334,000 sq km); population 1,900,000; capital, Brazzaville (pop. 156,000); currency, franc; official language, French.

The People's Republic of the Congo was a French colony before independence in 1960. It lies across the equator in western Africa, and has a short coastal plain on the Atlantic. Most of the country is high; the broad Batéké Plateau is savanna, but the northern region is covered with thick tropical forest. The Congo and Oubangui rivers form the eastern boundary. The chief crop is sugar-cane. There are various mineral resources.

DAHOMEY
Area 44,696 sq miles (115,762 sq km); population 2,940,000; capital, Porto Novo (pop. 85,000); currency, franc; official language, French.

Independent since 1960, Dahomey was previously a French colony. It is one of the most densely populated countries of western Africa. The centre of Dahomey is a high plateau, and there are lowlands in the north and south. The majority of the people live in the coastal region. Palm oil, coffee, tobacco, and cotton are exported.

EGYPT
Area 386,000 sq miles (999,700 sq km); population 35,500,000; capital, Cairo (pop. 5,300,000); currency, pound (100 piastres); official language, Arabic.

Egypt—now called the Arab Republic of Egypt—was a monarchy from 1923 to 1952. Earlier, it had been a British protectorate, and, until 1914, part of the Ottoman Empire. Though most of Egypt's territory is in Africa, a small section, the Sinai Peninsula, is in Asia. The Suez Canal passes through Egypt, and by connecting the Mediterranean Sea with the

EGYPT—The Sphinx at Gizeh

MOROCCO—A street in the old part of Fès

KENYA—A village market-place

SOUTH AFRICA—Cape Town and Table Mountain

The remains of the 5th-century basilica at Apollonia (Marsa Susa) in Libya. Apollonia was once the port for Cyrene (Shahat). Both the Greeks and the Romans left impressive relics of their colonization of the Mediterranean coast of northern Africa.

Left: The city of Marrakesch in Morocco, at the foot of the Atlas Mountains. Founded in the 11th century, it is the historical capital of southern Morocco. A caravan route led from it across the desert to Timbuktu.

Below: A nomad camp in the Sahara. Once, the nomads were the piratical lords of the desert, waylaying naravans and robbing oases—disappearing on their swift camels as fast as they had come. Today, the nomads that are left are mostly herdsmen or traders.

Red Sea provides a short route for shipping between Europe and Asia. Most of the land is desert: the Libyan Desert in the west, and the Arabian Desert in the east, rising to the Red Sea Mountains. Between the deserts is the valley of the Nile, the world's longest river. The Nile has no tributaries during the whole of its 900-mile (1,450-km) course through Egypt. Agriculture is possible only in the valley, and, in particular, in the great delta of the Nile on the Mediterranean. The amount of arable land has been increased by building dams for irrigation. The most important dam, the Aswan High Dam, has greatly aided Egypt's economy by the production of hydro-electricity as well as by making water available to farmers. Most of the people live in the valley; those in the desert live in oases or are nomads. Among the country's chief crops are cotton, sugar, citrus fruits, and rice.

EQUATORIAL GUINEA *Area 11,000 sq miles (28,000 sq km); population 300,000; capital, Malabo (Santa Isabel; pop. 9,000); currency, ekpwele; official language, Spanish.*

The small country of Equatorial Guinea consists largely of the former Spanish possessions of Rio Muni and Fernando Póo; it gained independence in 1968. Rio Muni is on the African mainland. Fernando Póo (Macias Nguema) is a mountainous island in the Gulf of Guinea. Cocoa and coffee are exported.

ETHIOPIA *Area 450,000 sq miles (1,165,000 sq km); population 26,000,000; capital, Addis Ababa (pop. 800,000); currency, dollar (100 cents); official language, Amharic.*

Until 1974, Ethiopia was ruled by an emperor who belonged to one of the oldest royal dynasties in the world; but in that year it became a republic. It is often called *Abyssinia.* Most of the country consists of high and broken plateaux, divided into two regions by the African Rift Valley. To the west of the valley are the Ethiopian Highlands, which are wild and rugged and are cut by many river valleys. To the east is the Somali Plateau, which is generally more level. The country has little industry, though it has some mineral resources including gold, platinum, and potash. Cereals, coffee, cotton, sugar-cane, fruit, and tobacco are grown; of these, coffee is the chief export product.

GABON *Area 103,100 sq miles (267,000 sq km); population 500,000; capital, Libreville (pop. 31,000); currency, franc; official language, French.*

Gabon has been independent since 1960. Before that, it was a French colony. Its coastal plain on the Atlantic is broad around the mouth of the River Ogooué. But most of the country is a mountainous plateau, which has extensive rain forests in which mahogany and other valuable timbers are cut. There are good crops of cocoa and coffee, and in recent years rice cultivation has begun. Gabon's mineral resources include oil, iron, and manganese.

GAMBIA *Area 4,000 sq miles (10,500 sq km); population 493,000; capital, Banjul (Bathurst; pop. 40,000); currency, dalasi (100 bututs); official language, English.*

The small country of Gambia was British-ruled before it became independent in 1966. It consists of a narrow strip of territory along the Gambia River. Some of the land is swampy or under water for part of the year. There are few mineral resources. The chief exports are ground-nuts and fruit.

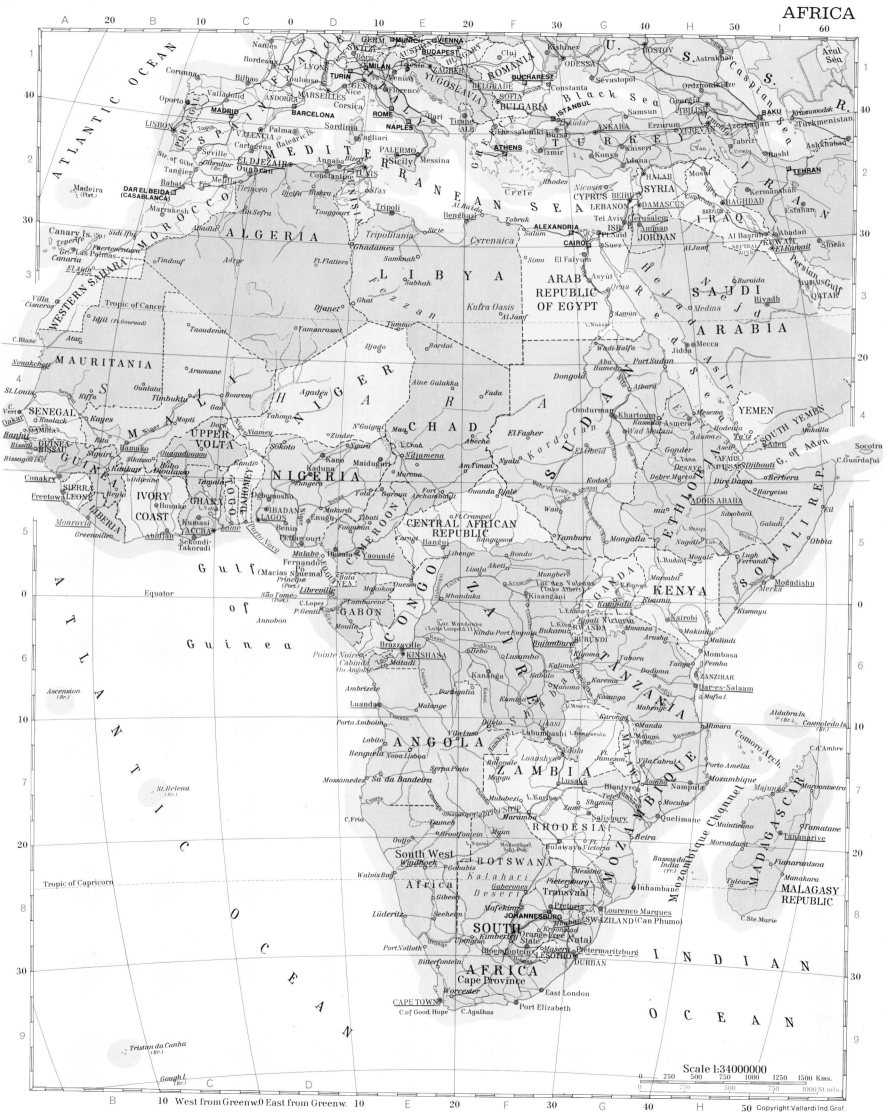

Dromedaries—one-humped riding camels—being watered in Nigeria. The camel, the 'ship of the desert', can walk a hundred miles without eating or drinking. In its dogged, unfriendly manner, it can carry a load of 350 pounds (160 kg) and cover 40 miles (65 km) a day. It owes its powers of endurance to its strange anatomy. It has a 'larder' inside its body. The camel stores a reserve of food in its hump as fat. It also stores water in its body. And, unlike most animals, it does not sweat and, consequently, does not lose water in this way. Until this century, it was almost the only means of transport in the desert. But even the camel has been overtaken by technology. Increasingly, it is being ousted by the motor vehicle.

GHANA *Area 92,100 sq miles (238,538 sq km); population 9,900,000; capital, Accra (pop. 900,000); currency, cedi (100 pesewas); official language, English.*

The former British colony of the Gold Coast, Ghana has been independent since 1957. Most of eastern Ghana is in the basin of the Volta River and, like the coastal areas, is low-lying. But there are hills in the east, and a high escarpment extends across the country. The building of the Akosombo Dam on the Volta has produced the largest artificial lake in the world, covering more than 3,000 sq miles (7,800 sq km). This project has aided irrigation and has provided much-needed electrical power. Gold, diamonds, manganese, and bauxite are mined, and there is an aluminium-smelting industry. The chief export crops are cocoa, coffee, and copra.

GUINEA *Area 96,900 sq miles (250,970 sq km); population 4,100,000; capital, Conakry (pop. 120,000); currency, franc; official language, French.*

Guinea, which became independent in 1958, was formerly a French colony. The land rises from the broad, marshy coastal plain on the Atlantic to the Fouta Djallon, a rugged plateau. In the south-east, the thickly forested Nimba Mountains rise to some 5,800 ft (1,800 m). The chief rivers are the Niger and the Gambia, both of which have their sources in Guinea. There are rich deposits of bauxite and iron. The chief export crops are bananas, pineapples, kola-nuts, and coffee.

GUINEA-BISSAU *Area 14,000 sq miles (36,000 sq km); population 580,000; capital, Bissau (pop. 65,000); currency, escudo (100 centavos).*

Until 1974 a Portuguese possession (called Portuguese Guinea), Guinea-Bissau consists of a mainland territory and a number of islands on the Atlantic coast of Africa. It is mostly low-lying, but the high plateau of the Fouta Djallon projects into the south-east. The chief crops are rice, ground-nuts, and palm oil.

IVORY COAST *Area 125,000 sq miles (323,700 sq km); population 4,600,000; capital, Abidjan (pop. 600,000); currency, franc; official language, French.*

Ivory Coast became independent in 1960;

The Sahara at Beni-Abbès in Algeria. In Arabic, the word *Sahara* means *desert*. This desert, the world's largest, stretches right across northern Africa from the Atlantic Ocean to the Red Sea. Some of it is sandy (*erg*, in Arabic), some rocky (*hammada*), and some stony (*serir*). In many places, it is flat and featureless, but it also has three mountain ranges. Here and there in the wastes are *oases*—patches of vegetation watered by springs of underground water.

previously it was a French colony. The northern two-thirds of the country is a savanna-covered plateau. The coastal plain is broad and wooded. The most valuable crops are cocoa and coffee; and bananas and pineapples are also exported. Timber is an important source of revenue.

KENYA *Area 224,960 sq miles (582,644 sq km); population 12,900,000; capital, Nairobi (pop. 510,000); currency, shilling (100 cents); official languages, English and Swahili.*

Kenya became independent in 1963; it had been a British colony since 1895. Much of the northern part of the country is a plateau, a region of wide grasslands. In the south-west, the Kenya Highlands include Kenya's two highest mountains, Mount Kenya (17,057 ft; 5,199 m) and Mount Elgon (14,177 ft; 4,321 m). The Nyanza Plateau, which stretches from the highlands to Lake Victoria, is one of the most favoured agricultural regions. The African Rift Valley cuts through Kenya; Lake Rudolf, in the north, lies within it. The lower parts of the country consist of dry and thorn savannas. The chief crops are sisal, cereals, pineapples, tea, and coffee. Pyrethrum is cultivated as a pesticide. Kenya is famous for its wild-life reserves.

LESOTHO *Area 11,716 sq miles (30,344 sq km); population 1,170,000; capital, Maseru (pop. 30,000); currency, rand (100 cents); official languages, English and Sesotho.*

Lesotho, the former British colony of Basutoland, is an enclave surrounded by the territory of South Africa. It became independent in 1966. Nearly all of the country is high; the Drakensberg Mountains rise in the east. The Orange River has its source in Lesotho. The raising of livestock is important.

LIBERIA *Area 43,000 sq miles (111,370 sq km); population 1,300,000; capital, Monrovia (pop. 110,000); currency, dollar (100 cents); official language, English.*

The Liberian republic was founded in 1847, and is the oldest independent country in western Africa. It developed from a number of settlements for Negroes released from slavery in the United States. The Guinea Highlands and Nimba Mountains in the north descend to savanna plateaux, and then to a marshy coastal plain. Iron and diamonds are mined. Crops include coffee and cocoa.

LIBYA *Area 679,360 sq miles (1,759,534 sq km); population 2,250,000; capital, Tripoli (pop. 550,000); currency, dinar (1,000 dirhams); official language, Arabic.*

Libya became an independent country in 1951. Earlier, it had been an Italian colony (from 1912) and, before that, part of the Ottoman Empire. It is one of the largest countries in Africa, but nine-tenths of it is barren land, part of the Sahara. Most of the people live in the fertile lowlands along the Mediterranean coast. This region has groves of oranges and olives, and also grows cereals, tobacco, and vegetables. The country is rich because of huge deposits of petroleum.

MALAGASY REPUBLIC *Area 230,000 sq miles (595,700 sq km); population 7,200,000; capital Tananarive (pop. 400,000); currency, franc; official languages, Malagasy and French.*

The Malagasy Republic occupies the island of Madagascar in the Indian Ocean, and a few other small islands. It is some 250 miles (400 km) from the coast of the African mainland. It was governed by France from 1885 to 1960.

The centre of Madagascar is a high plateau, bounded by mountains in the north and south, and by a wide coastal plain on the west. Only one-tenth of the land is suitable for agriculture. Exports include sugar, coffee, pepper, vanilla, and cloves. Graphite, mica, and phosphates are mined.

MALAWI *Area 45,500 sq miles (117,850 sq km); population 4,800,000; capital, Zomba (pop. 20,000); currency, kwacha (100 tambala); official language, English.*

The former British protectorate of Nyasaland, Malawi became an independent country in 1964. It lies along the western side of Lake Malawi (Lake Nyasa), which is in the African Rift Valley. Most of the people live by farming; and tea, tobacco, and tung-oil are exported. Cattle-rearing and fishing (on lake waters) are important.

MALI *Area 465,000 sq miles (1,204,000 sq km); population 5,100,000; capital, Bamako (pop. 170,000); currency, franc; official language, French.*

Mali was formerly the French colony of Soudan. In 1959 it joined with Senegal to form the Federation of Mali; but the federation was dissolved after a year, and Mali and Senegal became separate countries. The loss of Senegal left Mali without an outlet to the sea. The northern part of the country is in the Sahara and is almost uninhabited except for nomads. The south is watered by the Niger and Senegal rivers. Cotton and ground-nuts are exported.

MAURITANIA *Area 419,000 sq miles (1,085,000 sq km); population 1,250,000; capital, Nouakchott (pop. 30,000); currency, ouguiya (5 khoums); official language, Arabic.*

Mauritania became an independent country in 1960; it had been ruled by France since 1920. It is officially called the *Islamic Republic of Mauritania*. Much of the country is in the western Sahara and consists of barren plateaux. Only in the south-west, the flood plain of the Senegal River, is the land fertile. Cereals and ground-nuts are produced. The most important source of income is iron ore, which is of high quality.

MAURITIUS *Area 800 sq miles (2,000 sq km); population 861,000; capital, Port Louis (pop. 135,000); currency, rupee (100 cents); official languages, English, French, and Creole.*

The tiny country of Mauritius was a British crown colony until 1968. It consists of a group of islands in the Indian Ocean, the largest of which are Mauritius and Rodrigues. Mauritius Island is mountainous and is of volcanic origin. The main crop is sugar-cane.

MOROCCO *Area 171,000 sq miles (442,888 sq km); population 16,500,000; capital, Rabat (pop. 565,000); currency, dirham (100 centimes); official language, Arabic.*

Morocco became independent in 1956, after 44 years of rsle by France and Spain. During that time, the city of Tangier was an international zone under the control of France, Spain, and Britain. The country is dominated by the Atlas Mountains, which rise to 13,661 ft (4,164 m) above sea-level in Mount Toubkal. To the east of the mountains are the wastes of the Sahara. Morocco's coastal plain on the Mediterranean, in the north, is hilly, but the western, Atlantic coast has sandy beaches. The country has rich mineral deposits, and supplies a third of the

Above: Dancers at a village festival in Kenya. Throughout Africa, governments are trying to modernize their countries and improve living standards by means of technology. At the same time they are conscious of the need to protect and foster the continent's rich and varied cultural traditions—its music, dance, painting, and sculpture.

Right: The stark, eroded outline of Mount Kenya (17,057 ft; 5,199 m), Africa's second highest mountain. The peak is an extinct volcano, and its base has a diameter of 40 miles (65 km). Although Mount Kenya is almost on the equator, many glaciers move down its slopes.

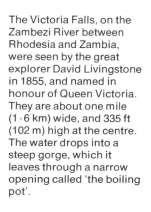

The Victoria Falls, on the Zambezi River between Rhodesia and Zambia, were seen by the great explorer David Livingstone in 1855, and named in honour of Queen Victoria. They are about one mile (1·6 km) wide, and 335 ft (102 m) high at the centre. The water drops into a steep gorge, which it leaves through a narrow opening called 'the boiling pot'.

Giraffes in a national park in Kenya. Kenya's nature reservations and national parks cover more than 23,000 sq miles (60,000 sq km), the most extensive conservation areas in the world. The variety of animal life in Africa is greater than in any other continent. But Africa's animals are in danger. Fifty years ago there were 20 times as many of them as there are today. One of the reasons for this decrease has been the shrinking of their living space. Forests and bush have been cleared for agriculture, land has been flooded to make artificial lakes, and roads have brought motor vehicles to regions that were wild only a few years ago. Hunters, too, have taken their toll, the quarry being the more valuable animals, such as elephants. In order to protect the continent's animals, several countries have established conservation areas. The killing of certain species of animals is punished severely.

A lion in a national park enjoys his dinner, ignoring the fascinated but awe-struck onlookers. Visitors to conservation areas must observe strict rules. They are not allowed to carry firearms, and they must not get out of the vehicles in which they are travelling. The animals seem to accept that visitors will not interfere with them. Apart from occasional mild curiosity, they act as though alone.

world demand for phosphates. Crops include cereals, oranges, olives, apricots, grapes (for wine as well as for eating), and nuts.

MOZAMBIQUE *Area 303,000 sq miles (705,000 sq km); population 8,233,000; capital, Can Phumo (Lourenço Marques; pop. 440,000); currency, escudo (100 centavos); official language, Portuguese.*

The People's Republic of Mozambique, independent since 1975, was formerly ruled by Portugal. It has a coastline of some 1,500 miles (2,400 km) on the Indian Ocean, and the great Lake Malawi (Lake Nyasa) is in the north. The country has a wide coastal plain, but most of it consists of highlands through which flow several important rivers, including the Zambezi and Limpopo. Cane-sugar, tea, cotton, and coconuts are produced. Coal and iron are mined.

NIGER *Area 459,000 sq miles (1,189,000 sq km); population 4,300,000; capital, Niamey (pop. 100,000); currency, franc; official language, French.*

Niger was ruled by France before independence in 1960. It has no coastline, and most of it is an arid plateau. The northern part is in the Sahara. A few small rivers seep away into the desert; they provide water for scattered patches of green. The south of the country is savanna, and in the south-west there is fertile land around the Niger River. Cereals, coffee, and cotton are grown, and there are deposits of tin, iron, and uranium.

NIGERIA *Area 356,669 sq miles (923,768 sq km); population 79,700,000; capital, Lagos (pop. 1,000,000); currency, naira (100 kobo); official language, English.*

Nigeria, the most heavily-populated country in Africa, was a British colony and protectorate until 1960. The chief feature of the country is the great Niger River, which, with its tributaries, waters most of Nigeria. There are mangrove swamps and lagoons along the coast, particularly in the Niger delta. Some 50 miles (80 km) inland the rain forest begins; beyond this are the plateaux, and, still farther north, a semi-desert tract. Lake Chad is on the north-east frontier. Two-thirds of Nigeria's agricultural produce is exported. The country is the leading producer of

ground-nuts in the world, and is among the leaders for cocoa. The rearing of stock, particularly cattle, is important. Petroleum is extracted, as well as tin and coal. There are food-processing and oil-refining industries, and textiles, steel, and chemicals are manufactured.

RHODESIA *Area 150,820 sq miles (390,622 sq km); population 5,800,000; capital, Salisbury (pop. 503,000); currency, dollar (100 cents); official language, English.*

Rhodesia is one of the few countries in Africa that has a government of white people. It was formerly the British colony of Southern Rhodesia; but in 1965 the colonial government declared the country independent in order to forestall a grant of independence by the British government that would lead to black majority rule. Rhodesia has no outlet to the sea. Most of it is a plateau lying between the basins of the Zambezi River in the north and the Limpopo River in the south-east. On the border with Zambia is Lake Kariba, formed by the building of the Kariba Dam, which supplies Rhodesia and Zambia with hydro-electricity. In the north-east, the land rises to the Rhodesian Highlands. Rhodesia has rich mineral resources, including iron, copper, asbestos, and gold. Its crops include tobacco, cereals, sugar-cane, and fruit. The raising of beef cattle is very important.

RWANDA *Area 10,169 sq miles (26,338 sq km); population 3,200,000; capital, Kigali (pop. 7,000); currency, franc; official languages, French and Kiswahili.*

Rwanda was, until 1962, part of the UN trust territory of Ruanda-Urundi, administered by Belgium. It is bounded on the west by Lake Kivu. Most of it occupies a hilly plateau. Mountains in the west, by the lake, divide the basin of the River Congo from that of the Nile. Coffee, tea, and tobacco are exported.

SENEGAL *Area 77,800 sq miles (201,500 sq km); population 4,000,000; capital, Dakar (pop. 581,000); currency, franc; official language, French.*

Senegal, a former French colony, became part of the Federation of Mali in 1959; but one year later the Federation was dissolved, and Senegal and Mali became separate countries. Cape Vert in Senegal is the westernmost point in Africa. The country has a long, sandy coast on the Atlantic Ocean, and is mostly low-lying. But in the south-east it has hills of the Fouta Djalon. Its rivers include the Senegal and the Gambia. Much of the valley of the Gambia River forms a separate country, called the Gambia, which is an enclave within Senegalese territory. The chief crops are rice and ground-nuts. Phosphates are mined.

SIERRA LEONE *Area 27,925 sq miles (72,325 sq km); population 2,600,000; capital, Freetown (pop. 128,000); currency, leone (100 cents); official language, English.*

Sierra Leone, which became independent in 1961, was formerly a British colony; the colony was founded around a settlement at Freetown for escaped slaves. Most of the country is high and mountainous, and consists of a broken plateau that rises to the Fouta Djalon. Freetown is built on a hilly peninsula, but the rest of the coastal region is low-lying and marshy. Nearly three-quarters of the people live by agriculture: palm kernels, coffee, and cocoa are exported. Sierra Leone has useful mineral deposits. They include diamonds, iron, and bauxite.

SOMALIA *Area 246,200 sq miles (637,700 sq km); population 2,900,000; capital, Mogadishu (pop. 220,000); currency, shilling (100 cents); official language, Somali.*

Somalia became an independent country in 1960; it was formed from two British and Italian possessions. It lies on the 'horn' of Africa, and has coastlines on the north, and the east, where the coastal plain is broad. The interior of the country is a plateau, sloping upwards towards the Ethiopian Highlands in the west. Bananas are exported, and other crops include cereals, ground-nuts, and cotton.

SOUTH AFRICA *Area 472,360 sq miles (1,223,410 sq km); population 21,500,000; capitals, Cape Town (legislative capital, pop. 1,100,000) and Pretoria (administrative capital, pop. 562,000); currency, rand (100 cents); official languages, English and Afrikaans.*

South Africa is the richest and the most southerly country in Africa. It is governed by its white population, which, although large, is only about one-fifth of the total population. The government pursues a policy of *apartheid* or *separate development* for the two sections of the community. The white people of South Africa are mainly of British or Dutch descent; those of Dutch ancestry are called *Afrikaners*. Most of the country consists of plateau land. The eastern plateau, the High Veld, is the most prosperous part of the country, with rich farmlands and highly-developed industry. It also has important mineral resources. To the south-east of the High Veld is the great mountain range of the Drakensbergs, and beyond that is a coastal plain. Two other large plateaux are called *karroos*—the Great Karroo in the south, and the Upper Karroo in the west. In the far north-east of the country is the *Transvaal*—the region 'beyond the Vaal River'. There are two other large rivers, the Limpopo and the Orange. South Africa's farms are among the most productive in the world. Their crops include cereals, vegetables, fruit, tobacco, and sugar-cane. Livestock, particularly sheep, are important. Vineyards produce fine wines. Textiles, steel, chemicals, and machinery are manufactured. About half of the gold mined in the world comes from South Africa. Diamonds, silver, iron, manganese, and chromium are also extracted.

SOUTH-WEST AFRICA *Area 318,261 sq miles (824,292 sq km); population 670,000; capital, Windhoek (pop. 60,000); currency, rand (100 cents); official languages, English and Afrikaans.*

Sometimes called *Namibia*, the large territory of South-West Africa is administered by South Africa, to which it was mandated by the League of Nations in 1920. The coastal area, called the *Namib*, is desert. Inland there is a vast plateau. Much of the country is too dry for crop cultivation, but there are large herds of livestock. Fishing is important, and there are mineral deposits.

SPANISH SAHARA *Area 120,000 sq miles (311,000 sq km); population 63,000; capital, El Aiún; currency, peseta; official language, Spanish.*

The vast territory of Spanish Sahara in north-west Africa constitutes an overseas province of Spain. It is mostly desert land, but has rich deposits of phosphates.

SUDAN *Area 967,500 sq miles (2,505,800 sq km); population 17,000,000; capital, Khartoum (pop. 135,000); currency, pound (100 piastres); official language, Arabic.*

The Sudan, the largest country in Africa, was ruled by Egypt from 1820 to 1880, and was under joint British and Egyptian rule from 1898 to 1956. The Nile and its tributaries reach out into almost all parts of the country. The Blue Nile and the White Nile meet at Khartoum, and flow northwards to Egypt. Northern Sudan is desert. South of the desert are hills, and beyond them broad plains of scrubby grassland and savanna. The southern parts of the country, near the equator, have rich vegetation, with alluvial grasslands, tropical forests, and swamp forests. Cotton and other crops are grown in the Nile valley, and irrigation works have aided agriculture along the Atbara River. Cereals, fruits, ground-nuts, and sugar-cane are produced. In the drier regions, cattle, sheep, goats, and camels are raised on a nomadic or semi-nomadic basis. Fishing is important, both in the Nile and on the Red Sea coast. Most of the people of northern Sudan are Arabs; in the south, many are Negroes.

SWAZILAND *Area 6,704 sq miles (17,363 sq km); population 460,000; capital, Mbabane (pop. 21,000); currency, rand (100 cents); official languages, English and Siswati.*

Swaziland became an independent country in 1968. At that time it was a British protectorate. The Lebombo Mountains rise along the eastern side of the country. The rest of the terrain is veld, higher in the west than elsewhere. Crops include sugar-cane, citrus fruits, cotton, and rice. Iron, asbestos, and gold are mined.

TANZANIA *Area 362,820 sq miles (939,700 sq km); population 14,000,000; capital, Dar es Salaam (pop. 300,000); currency, shilling (100 cents); official languages, Swahili and English.*

The United Republic of Tanzania was formed in 1964, its territory being the former

The scenery of southern Africa is extremely varied. The Blind River Canyon is a valley of extraordinary and unexpected beauty.

A village in Cameroon. The most usual dwelling in an African village is a hut of dried mud with a straw roof. Such a house provides all the shelter necessary in the circumstances of village life: lodging for the night, and protection against the rains. In the daytime, life is passed almost entirely in the open; there, food is cooked and meals are eaten. Often, a number of huts—perhaps the property of a large family—are enclosed by a wall. Within this enclosure, all the family property is kept. Partitions mark off a space for the domestic animals.

Left: Villagers in Ghana pounding cassava in a wooden mortar. Over much of Africa, people eat mainly cassava, maize (corn), millet, beans, sweet potatoes, and bananas. They eat meat very rarely. Though there are many cattle in some parts of Africa, they are kept mainly for their milk. A man's wealth is often reckoned in the number of animals he owns; consequently, animals are not slaughtered for food.

Fishermen in Kenya. Three-quarters of Africa's people live on food produced in their immediate neighbourhood. Along the coasts, and near lakes and rivers, fish are an important article of diet.

Coptic priests in Addis Ababa, the capital of Ethiopia. Christianity came to Ethiopia in the 4th century. It has remained the state religion, in the form of the Coptic Church. But there are other religions, too, including Judaism and Islam. Although the Catholic Church was established at an early date in northern Africa, it was not until relatively recently that Catholic and Protestant missionaries, along with European settlers, introduced Christianity to most of Negro Africa. There—in the past as in the present—religions existed that had their centre in animals, plants, or natural phenomena believed to have benign or malignant powers. Islam, too, is widespread in Africa. The Arabs and the Berbers are Muslims, and Islam is winning more and more adherents among the peoples of Africa south of the Sahara.

British trust territory of Tanganyika in eastern Africa, and some offshore islands of which the largest are Zanzibar and Pemba. On the northern and western frontiers of continental Tanzania there are three great lakes; Victoria, Tanganyika, and Malawi (Nyasa). Most of the country is a hilly plateau, forested in places and covered with scrubby grassland in others. In the north-east of the plateau is Mount Kilimanjaro (19,340 ft; 5,895 m), Africa's highest mountain. The coastal plain is narrow at most points. About a quarter of the land area has been declared nature conservation territory. The mainland has poor soils, but has a very large trade in sisal. Other crops include cereals, coffee, tea, and cotton.

TOGO *Area 21,853 sq miles (56,599 sq km); population 2,100,000; capital, Lomé (pop. 148,000); currency, franc; official language, French.*

The small country of Togo became independent in 1960; earlier it had been a French trusteeship territory, and, until 1919, a German protectorate. Much of the country is mountainous and thickly forested, but there is savanna in the north-west. The coastal districts are swampy, with large land-locked lagoons. The people grow some cereals, cassava, and yams. Cocoa, citrus fruits, palm kernels, and coffee are produced for export.

TUNISIA *Area 45,000 sq miles (116,500 sq km); population 5,600,000; capital, Tunis (pop. 1,127,000); currency, dinar (1,000 millimes); official language, Arabic.*

A French protectorate from 1883, Tunisia became completely independent in 1956. It is one of the smallest countries of northern Africa, and has the continent's most northerly point, Cape Blanc. The northern part of Tunisia is in the Atlas Mountains, which here rise to a maximum of some 5,000 ft (1,500 m) above sea-level. In the north-east there is a coastal plain. The southern region is in the Sahara. In the west is the vast salt pan called the *Chott Djerid*, which in the rainy season turns into a salty marsh. Vines, olives, vegetables, and citrus fruits grow in the Mediterranean region. In the desert, people live in the oases, and nomads keep animals.

UGANDA *Area 93,981 sq miles (243,410 sq km); population, 10,600,000; capital, Kampala (pop. 331,000); currency, shilling (100 cents); official language, English.*

The former British protectorate of Uganda became an independent country in 1962. It is an inland country, with no access to the sea. In the south-east, it includes part of Lake Victoria, Africa's largest lake. In the west, there are three other large lakes, Albert, George, and Edward. Most of the country is a high plateau, bordered on the east and the west by mountains. In the east, Mount Elgon rises to 14,178 ft (4,321 m); and in the west, Mount Stanley in the Ruwenzori Mountains rises to 16,794 ft (5,119 m). The chief river is the White Nile. The principal export crops are coffee, cotton, tea, fruit, ground-nuts, and sugar. Copper and tin are exported, too.

UPPER VOLTA *Area 105,869 sq miles (274,199 sq km); population 5,550,000; capital, Ouagadougou (pop. 125,000); currency, franc; official language, French.*

The former French colony of Upper Volta became an independent country in 1960. It lies on a sloping plateau, and has the headstreams of the Volta River—the Black, White, and Red Voltas. Despite its rivers, the country has an acute shortage of water, and its soil is poor. The typical vegetation is savanna. Nearly all the people live by farming, generally at subsistence level. The chief cash crops are ground-nuts and sesame. Considerable numbers of cattle and other livestock are kept, and the export of meat to neighbouring countries is an important source of income.

ZAIRE *Area 905,565 sq miles (2,345,402 sq km); population 18,600,000; capital, Kinshasa (formerly Léopoldville; pop. 1,300,000); currency, zaire (100 makuta); official language, French.*

The country was formerly called the *Republic of the Congo*. It was a Belgian colony that gained independence in 1960. Most of the country is a plateau, highest in the southeast, in Katanga. The eastern border, in the African Rift Valley, runs through several great lakes. This part is very mountainous, the Ruwenzori Mountains rising to 16,794 ft (5,119 m). The Zaire (Congo) River pursues a course of some 2,800 miles (4,500 km) through the country. Zaire is rich in minerals, particularly in copper. Diamonds, cobalt, and iron are among the other minerals extracted. Agricultural exports include coffee, tea, sugar, cotton, rubber, and fruit. There are many manufacturing industries.

ZAMBIA *Area 288,130 sq miles (746,253 sq km); population 4,700,000; capital, Lusaka (pop. 348,000); currency, kwacha (100 ngwee); official language, English.*

Zambia, which became independent in 1964, was formerly the British protectorate of Northern Rhodesia. The country is watered by one of Africa's great rivers, the Zambezi. Most of Zambia is a plateau, averaging some 4,000 ft (1,200 m) above sea-level. But some of the country is higher. The Muchinga Mountains in the eastern part rise to more than 7,000 ft (2,130 m). There are many lakes, either in Zambia or on its borders. They include Lake Kariba, in the south, an artificial lake formed by the building of the Kariba Dam. This project supplies hydro-electricity to Rhodesia as well as to Zambia. The country is rich in mineral resources, especially copper. The chief export crops are cereals, ground-nuts, tea, coffee, and cane sugar, but output is affected by high wages paid in mining.

NORTH & CENTRAL AMERICA

The honour was not given to Christopher Columbus, who was looking for the western sea route to India and discovered America instead, to confer his name on the new continent. This guarantee of fame fell to a Florentine seafarer and explorer, Amerigo Vespucci, who investigated and described the coastlines of the newly discovered land masses, a few years after Columbus. It was his Christian name that was used to christen America.

The Americas consist of two continents connected together by a narrow land bridge. North and Central America, which geographers refer to simply as North America, embraces a somewhat larger area than South America, and is two-and-a-half times as large as Europe. It has, very roughly, the shape of an equilateral triangle, the south-western apex of which is somewhat bent. The northern side of this triangle presents a highly indented coastline, off which lie numerous islands. Geographically and geologically speaking, the largest island in the world, Greenland, which is administered by Denmark, also belongs to North America.

In the east of North America, along the Atlantic coastline, stretches the Appalachian Range of mountains. On the western side of America, mighty ranges of high mountains traverse the whole continent. Their highest peak, the 20,320-foot (6,194-metre) Mt McKinley, is in Alaska. One chain of mountains runs close to the coast, and is known by various names. The range lying more to the east is the Rocky Mountains, called in Mexico the Sierra Madre Oriental. Between these imposing mountain ranges on opposite sides of the continent, plains extend broadly from Hudson Bay in the north as far as the Gulf of Mexico.

Geologists have established the fact that America and Asia were once connected together by a firm land bridge—where the Bering Strait is found today. Mongolian tribes used this route some 20,000 years ago to travel from Asia to the American continent. Their descendants are North America's oldest inhabitants, and it was they whom the Spaniards confronted when

UNITED STATES—New York City from the East River, with UN building in foreground

they made their first landing. As the latter thought they were in India, they named these peoples accordingly. In a war of conquest that lasted for many years, the Whites destroyed many of the Indian tribes, and the highly developed culture of the Mexican Indians was brought to ruins.

In North America, the White settlers drove the hunting tribes from their hunting grounds. The survivors were finally given reservations in the United States and Canada. In all, there are today scarcely a million of the original inhabitants left. And as the total population of North America is reckoned at more than 300 million, it is correct to say that America is a land of immigrants and their descendants. Among these, Europeans are by far the majority. The Spaniards and Portuguese came first,

to Mexico, Florida, and the tropical regions, in search of gold and silver. Next came the French, and they settled in Canada and Louisiana. Later came the Dutch and the Swedes. In the 17th century began the great wave of emigration of Anglo-Saxon would-be settlers. These founded the first colonies in Virginia and New England, and spread out towards the west and the north.

Negroes also came to America, but, in contrast to the Whites, they came as slaves. They were taken from their African homelands to work on the cotton and tobacco plantations in the fertile south of the United States and the islands of the Caribbean, where today they are even in a majority on certain islands. In the United States, there are about 23 million Negroes.

USA—Heads of US presidents carved out of rock at Mount Rushmore, South Dakota

USA—The famous Manhattan skyline, New York harbour

USA—Fields of wheat on the Interior Plains
CANADA—Horseshoe Falls, Niagara

BAHAMAS *Area 5,400 sq miles (13,990 sq km); population 193,000; capital, Nassau (pop. 112,000); currency, dollar (100 cents); official language, English.*

The Bahamas were a British colony from 1649 to 1964, when they became self-governing. They acquired their independence in 1973. The whole group of islands is strung out between Florida and Haiti, and consists of some 700 islands, about 25 of which are inhabited, and over 2,000 reefs and keys. Thanks to the excellent climate, the Bahamas are a great attraction for foreign tourist traffic. The native population consists almost entirely of coloured peoples.

BARBADOS *Area 166 sq miles (430 sq km); population 241,000; capital, Bridgetown (pop. 19,000); currency, dollar (100 cents); official language, English.*

Barbados became a British colony in 1652, attained self-government in 1961, and won its independence in 1966. It is the most easterly island of the Lesser Antilles, and has a tropical and humid climate. The fertile soil is given over almost exclusively to the production of sugar-cane. Tourism is the second most important industry.

BELIZE *Area 8,900 sq miles (23,000 sq km); population 120,000; capital, Belmopan (pop. 5,000); currency, dollar (100 cents); official language, English.*

A British colony as British Honduras since 1884, Belize became a self-governing dependency in 1964. It lies on the Caribbean coast of Central America, to the east of Guatemala. The population is made up largely of Negroes and people of mixed blood, along with about 3,000 Whites and several thousand American Indians. Wood, sugar, and citrus fruits are the most important exports.

BERMUDA *Area 21 sq miles (53 sq km); population 60,000; capital, Hamilton (pop. 2,000); currency, dollar (100 cents); official language, English.*

Bermuda, a group of some 350 small islands in the Atlantic, 580 miles (930 km) from the United States, became a British colony in 1684, and a self-governing dependency in 1968. About 20 of the islands are inhabited, and tourism is the most important source of income.

CANADA *Area 3,851,809 sq miles (9,976,139 sq km); population 21,568,000; capital, Ottawa (pop. 536,000); currency, dollar (100 cents); official languages, English and French.*

After the USSR, Canada is the next largest country in the world. It is, however, relatively thinly populated, and still welcomes immigration. For more than a hundred years, the English and French fought over the possession of this land. The last battle was won by the British in 1759, and in 1763 France resigned all her claims. The French settlers were, however, permitted to remain in the country and retain their own language. In the province of Quebec, the French Canadians still constitute a nlosed racial group. Canada has been a member of the British Empire and Commonwealth since 1867, but although the British monarch reigns as monarch of Canada, the country is completely independent and self-governing.

In a north-south direction, Canada stretches for some 2,900 miles (4,670 km). As a result, the climate is extremely varied. A narrow coastal strip in the west has a mild maritime climate, whereas in the interior there is a dry and cold continental climate. North of the Arctic Circle, snow lies on the ground almost the whole year through, whereas in Ontario, on Canada's southern border, the vine is cultivated.

About half of Canada is taken up by a land region known as the Canadian Shield. Sparsely populated and made up of hard, ancient rocks, this horseshoe-shaped region stretches down central Canada from the Northwest Territories, round Hudson Bay to the northern coast of Quebec. A swampy, forested lowland separates the Shield from the southern shores of Hudson Bay, and to the east there are the Appalachian region (Newfoundland, Nova Scotia, etc.) and the St Lawrence-Great Lakes lowlands. The latter is a comparatively small region, but more than half the country's people live there. Its flat and rolling land is extremely fertile. West of the Shield are the interior plains (the prairies, where Canada's vast output of wheat is grown), and the western mountain region, which contains the Canadian Rockies and the Coast Mountains. Canada also has a number of very large islands, which lie almost entirely within the Arctic Circle.

Canada has vast mineral resources in the west, and more recently, oil and natural gas have been found, principally in the centre of the south-west. But although industry is in a leading position in the economy, Canada still remains a land of fishermen, hunters, and farmers. Almost half the land area is covered with forest. Thus, in addition to the trapping and farming of fur-bearing animals, the timber, furniture, and paper industries are very highly developed.

Three-quarters of Canada's people live in the towns. Only small groups of the original inhabitants of the country are still extant: Some 20,000 Eskimoes and 250,000 American Indians (most of whom live on reservations). All others are descendants of immigrants.

COSTA RICA *Area 19,650 sq miles (50,890 sq km); population 1,800,000; capital, San José (pop. 216,000); currency, colón (100 centimos); official language, Spanish.*

Originally a colony of Spain, Costa Rica has been an independent republic since 1821. It lies on the land bridge between North and South America, bordering in the north-east on the Caribbean and in the south-west on the Pacific. Its main products are coffee, sugar, and bananas.

CUBA *Area 44,218 sq miles (114,524 sq km); population 8,553,000; capital, Havana (pop. 1,755,000); currency, peso (100 centavos); official language, Spanish.*

Discovered by Christopher Columbus in 1492, Cuba was a Spanish possession until it became an independent republic in 1898. A revolution in the 1950s saw the communist Fidel Castro come to power in 1959.

A beautiful island, the largest in the Greater Antilles, Cuba lies between Florida and Jamaica. Three-quarters of its inhabitants are Whites, mostly of Spanish descent, while the rest are Negroes or of mixed blood. The 2,100-mile (3,400-km) coastline has many small bays, and numbers of minor islands and coral reefs lie just off it. The eastern part of the island is mountainous, the maximum height being 6,560 feet (2,000 metres). The

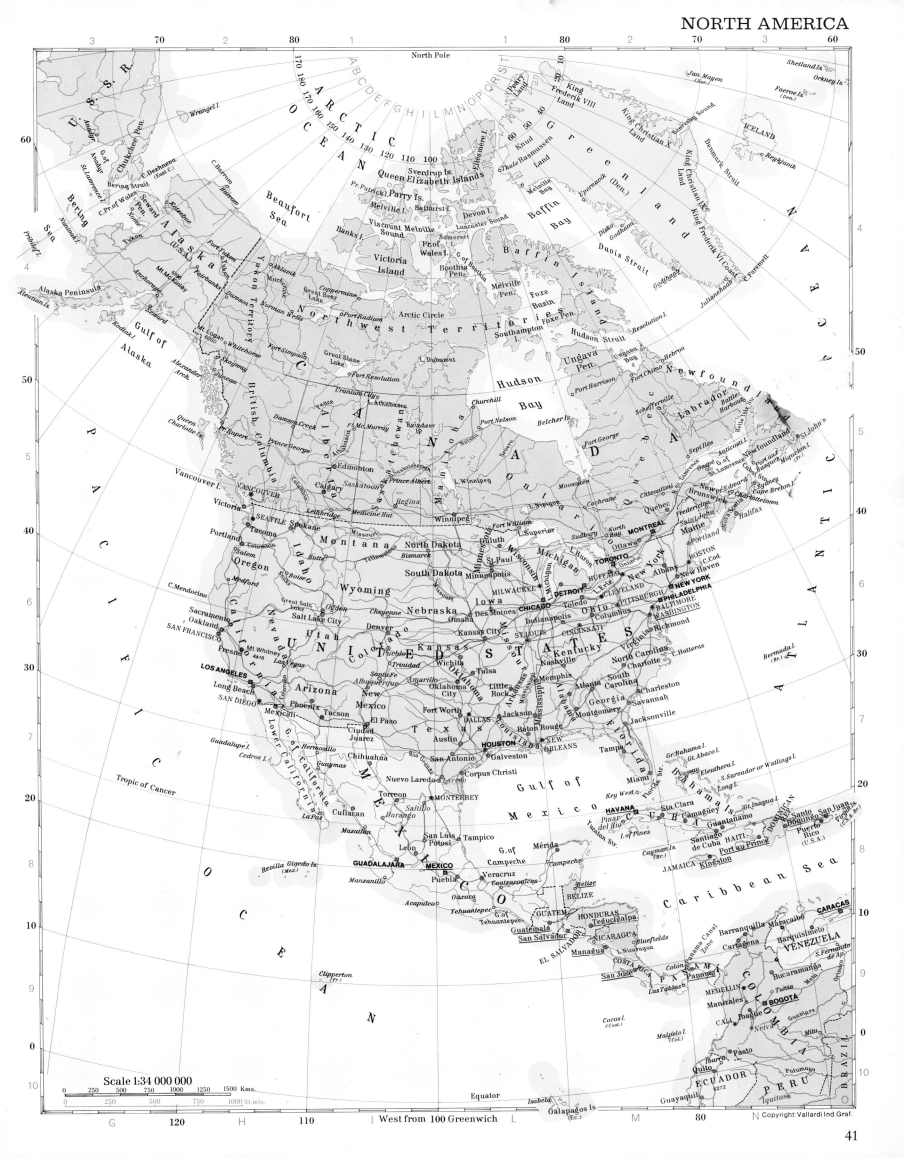

Scale 1:34 000 000

rest is flat or rolling land. Cuba is the world's second largest producer of sugar. Tobacco is also an important crop, and there are large reserves of nickel.

DOMINICAN REPUBLIC *Area 18,800 sq miles (48,700 sq km); population 4,012,000; capital, Santo Domingo (pop. 817,000); currency, peso (100 centavos); official language, Spanish.*

The Dominican Republic has been independent since 1844, after periods of Spanish and French possession. It occupies two-thirds of the island of Hispaniola, which lies in the West Indies between Cuba and Puerto Rico. About two-thirds of the population are Mulattoes (of mixed White/Negro blood), the rest being Whites or Negroes. A central mountain range rises to heights of 10,000 feet (3,000 metres) in the west, on the frontier with Haiti. In the fertile eastern plains, sugar-cane, coffee, and cacao are grown. Mineral resources include bauxite.

EL SALVADOR *Area 8,260 sq miles (21,400 sq km); population 3,541,000; capital, San Salvador (pop. 337,000); currency, colón (100 centavos); official language, Spanish.*

The smallest but the most thickly populated of the Central American states, El Salvador has been an independent republic since 1841. From a narrow, hot and humid coastal strip, the land rises to a volcanic mountain region, a 2,000-foot (600-metre) plateau, and another mountain range. Rice, maize, and coffee are the most important agricultural products. About three-quarters of the people are Mestizos (of mixed White/American Indian blood) and a fifth are American Indians.

GREENLAND *Area 840,000 sq miles (2,175,000 sq km); population 50,000; capital, Godthåb (pop. 8,000).*

Greenland, which lies to the north-east of North America, is the largest island in the world. Colonized at various times by Denmark and Norway, it became a province of Denmark in 1953 with equal rights with the rest of the country. About 85 per cent of its surface is covered by a permanent layer of thick ice. After Antarctica, it is the largest frozen expanse of land in the world. A mountainous coastal strip surrounding the ice-cap is free of ice, and has been strongly indented by fjords to form a number of small islands and peninsulas. The highest peak rises 12,139 feet (3,700 metres). Most Greenlanders have both Eskimo and Danish ancestry. They speak Greenlandic, a form of Eskimo language, and many also speak Danish. The main occupations are fishing and the processing of fish.

GRENADA *Area 133 sq miles (344 sq km); population 105,000; capital, St George's (pop. 8,400); currency, dollar (100 cents); official language, English.*

An island of the Lesser Antilles group, Grenada became an independent nation within the Commonwealth in 1974.

GUATEMALA *Area 42,040 sq miles (108,900 sq km); population 5,400,000; capital, Guatemala City (pop. 790,000); currency, quetzal (100 centavos); official language, Spanish.*

The most populous of the Central American

Alaska. *Above:* The Alaska Range, with Mount McKinley, the highest peak in North America, in the background. *Left:* Fishing in winter. When the United States purchased Alaska from Russia in 1867, many Americans were of the opinion that their country had paid too high a price for this lonely country. But then gold and, later, oil were discovered, and the fishing along the coast also proved to be exceedingly profitable. A further advantage, found later, was that the region makes an excellent military base, facing Russia as it does. Thus the sceptics were silenced. In this gigantic land, which has still not been completely opened up by roads and railways, the aeroplane is of primary importance. It is for this reason that, relative to its population, Alaska has more aircraft than any other place in the world.

Left: The Changing of the Guard, in front of the Parliament Building in Ottawa, the capital of Canada. The influence of England is reflected not only in the architecture of many of Canada's public buildings, but also in such minor ways as the uniform worn by certain army regiments. The French also settled in parts of the country, and traditions of both of these races are still alive today in the Canadians' way of life. About 45 per cent of the population of Canada is of British origin and nearly 30 per cent of French origin.

states, Guatemala, once a Spanish colony, has been independent since 1821. It has a long history of political troubles. The land is volcanic, and has a tropical climate. Coffee is grown in the fertile mountain districts, and bananas and cotton are also important. About 45 per cent of the people are American Indians. Most of the others follow Spanish-American customs and are known as *Ladinos*.

HAITI *Area 10,700 sq miles (27,700 sq km); population 4,768,000; capital, Port au Prince (pop. 300,000); currency, gourde (100 centimes); official language, French.*

Haiti, today an independent republic, has been a Spanish and French colony in turn, and was, from 1915 to 1934, under the control of the United States. It occupies the western third of the island of Hispaniola, and is the poorest and most backward country of Central America. It has a long history of uprisings and revolutions. The majority of the inhabitants are Negroes, the descendants of slaves. They speak a creole dialect, and practise voodoo. The small ruling class is made up largely of Mulattoes. The land is mountainous, only a third of it being arable. Coffee and sugar are the most important products.

HONDURAS *Area 43,300 sq miles (112,000 sq km); population 2,535,000; capital, Tegucigalpa (pop. 225,000); currency, lempira (100 centavos); official language, Spanish.*

Formerly under Spanish control, Honduras declared its independence in 1838. it lies in northern Central America, on the Caribbean, with a short Pacific coastline in the south. The interior is mountainous, and much of the coastal area is swamp and jungle. Most of the people are of mixed blood, and earn their living on the land. The most important products are bananas and coffee.

JAMAICA *Area 4,400 sq miles (11,400 sq km); population 1,935,000; capital, Kingston (pop. 573,000); currency, dollar (100 cents); official language, English.*

A former British colony, Jamaica became independent in 1962. It is the southernmost island of the Greater Antilles group. The interior is mountainous, and the Blue Mountains in the east rise to a height of 7,402 feet (2,256 metres). There are frequent earthquakes, one of which almost wholly destroyed the capital in 1907. In the fertile coastal plain to the west of Kingston, the principal crop grown is sugar-cane. Jamaica is the world's largest producer of bauxite (aluminium ore), and its rum is regarded as the finest in the world.

MEXICO *Area 760,000 sq miles (1,968,000 sq km); population 48,313,000; capital, Mexico City (pop. 8,000,000); currency, peso (100 centavos); official language, Spanish.*

Mexico was a Spanish possession until its independence in 1821. Today it is a republic consisting of 29 federal states. The largest Central American country, it lies between the Pacific and the Gulf of Mexico, and borders the United States in the north. The Sierra Madre, an extension of the Rocky Mountains, stretches down from the north in two long chains through the whole of Mexico. Between them lies an elevated plateau, where most of the people live. On the southern edge of this

Above: Monument Valley in Utah, one of the western United States. This huge, desert-like region with its extensive eroded landscape lies in the middle of the Rocky Mountains, and is part of the Navajo Indian Reservation. The 'monuments' are red sandstone formations that rise several hundred feet from the flat valley floor.

The original inhabitants of North America were Amerindians, known as 'Red Indians' or 'redskins', probably on account of their war-paint; their skin is actually brown. Today, some 500,000 of them live in special 'reservations', isolated from the rest of the population. There they attempt to keep up the customs and ways of life of their forefathers, as can be seen in this camp (*right*). Most Amerindians are exceedingly poor, and although notionally they have equal rights and opportunities with other North American people, in practice it is difficult for them to join the mainstream of modern life.

Right: Death Valley, California, between the Sierra Nevada and the border with Nevada, is part of the Death Valley National Monument. It was named for its desolate environment by pioneers who crossed it in the mid-1800s. Many died there during the California gold rush of 1849. Death Valley is a deep trough about 130 miles (210 km) long. It contains the place with the lowest elevation in the western hemisphere, Badwater, which is 282 feet (86 metres) below sea level.

Above: Downtown Chicago, the second largest city in the United States. Situated on the shores of Lake Michigan, Chicago is the industrial and business centre of the Middle West. It is also the transportation centre of the United States, and a leading international port, with access to the sea by way of the St Lawrence Seaway.

Below: An Apollo spacecraft on the launching pad of Cape Canaveral (Cape Kennedy), Florida. The American Apollo space programme, a comprehensive assault on the Moon, began disastrously when three astronauts died in the Apollo I launch-pad fire in 1967. This series of space tests, however, turned out to be the most spectacular and successful of man's exploration of other worlds, culminating in the triumphant first manned landing on the Moon in 1969 (Apollo II) and five further manned explorations of our natural satellite.

plateau lie a series of volcanoes, some still active. The highest peak is Orizaba, which rises 18,701 feet (5,700 metres). The long arm of Lower California extends in the west, separated from the rest of the country by the Gulf of California. In the east of Mexico is the Yucatán Peninsula, a low limestone plateau. Many famous ruins of the ancient Maya Indian civilization are located there.

Mexico still has some three million pure-blooded American Indians, but most of the people are Mestizos. About three-quarters of the working population is engaged in agriculture, although only an eighth of the land is arable. The country has rich mineral resources. Gold and silver have always been found there, and there are also iron, copper, lead, uranium, and, above all, oil and natural gas. These, of course, form the foundation for the rapidly developing manufacturing industries.

NICARAGUA *Area 57,150 sq miles (148,020 sq km); population 2,300,000; capital, Managua (pop. 350,000); currency, córdoba (100 centavos); official language, Spanish.*

Nicaragua was a Spanish colony until 1821, and became an independent republic in 1838. It lies between Honduras and Costa Rica, and is the most thinly populated state in Central America. About 70 per cent of the inhabitants are Mestizos, and the rest are Whites, Negroes, or American Indians. The volcanic mountain region of the interior rises to a height of some 7,000 feet (2,100 metres). The swampy land on the Caribbean is known as the 'Mosquito Coast'. Forests cover four-fifths of the land, and only about a tenth is used for agriculture. The main crops are cotton, coffee, and sugar. Meat is also exported, and there are important deposits of gold and silver.

PANAMA *Area 29,200 sq miles (75,600 sq km); population 1,428,000; capital, Panama City (pop. 418,000); currency, balboa (100 cents); official language, Spanish.*

A small country that forms the narrow land bridge between North and South America, Panama is mountainous, with tropical rain forests, and is divided in two by the Panama Canal. Until 1903, Panama formed part of Colombia, but, with the support of the United States, it declared its independence once the Canal had been built. Much of the population finds employment in connection with the Canal. Important products include bananas and rice.

PUERTO RICO *Area 3,400 sq miles (8,800 sq km); population 2,900,000; capital, San Juan (pop. 851,000).*

An island of the Greater Antilles group, Puerto Rico belonged to Spain for nearly 400 years before being ceded to the United States in 1898. It is not one of the United States, but its inhabitants, who speak Spanish, have the rights of US citizens. The island is thickly populated and poor, which means that many emigrate to the United States. The economy is based on manufacturing and tourism as well as on agriculture.

UNITED STATES OF AMERICA *Area 3,615,211 sq miles (9,363,353 sq km); population 210,404,000; capital, Washington DC (pop. 2,861,000); currency, dollar (100 cents); official language, English.*

The United States is a federation of 50 states. The first 13 declared their independence in 1776, after emerging victorious in wars against their colonial masters, Britain and France. The United States is one of the largest and most powerful countries in the world. In the north, it has a long frontier with Canada, the eastern boundary is the Atlantic Ocean, the Pacific Ocean forms the western boundary, and the southern border is with Mexico and on the Gulf of Mexico. Alaska, the 49th state, lies to the west of Canada, and Hawaii, the 50th, lies in the Pacific, some 2,400 miles (3,860 km) west of California.

The mainland may be divided into five natural regions: (1) the Atlantic coastal plain, which gives way in the west to (2) a highland region—the long range of the Appalachians; the land then falls away again to (3) the broad interior plains crossed in a north-south direction by the Mississippi and the Missouri; (4) the western highlands consist of the rocky mountains, with their high plateaux and peaks of over 13,000 feet (4,000 metres), the Sierra Nevada, and other ranges; and (5) the coastal strip along the Pacific, which descends to the Ocean. Despite the size and variety of the country, most parts of the United States have a moderate climate.

The population is about 87 per cent Whites (descendants of immigrants and new immigrants themselves from all the countries of Europe), 11 per cent Negroes (mostly descendants of African slaves), and the others include some half million American Indians, most of whom live on reservations.

The United States is the richest country in the world. A high average standard of living is aimed at, and much is done to provide equality of opportunity, but a small minority still live in varying degrees of poverty. It is especially the negroes who stand, for the most part, on the lowest rung of the economic ladder.

It is mainly in the north that are found America's giant industrial undertakings. Industrialization has also extended to agriculture, and the working of the frequently huge farms is extensively mechanized and

Right: The majestic Golden Gate Bridge spans the harbour opening at the entrance to San Francisco Bay, on the west coast of the United States. San Francisco is the leading port on the Pacific Coast, and one of the world's most beautiful cities, but over it hangs the ever-present threat of an earthquake. It stands directly over a fault in the earth's crust, and in 1906 was completely devastated by a severe earth tremor.

specialized. Nowhere else on earth is so much maize, oats, tobacco, cotton, soya bean, and citrus fruit produced as in the United States. High productivity is also recorded for wheat, barley, and sugar-beet. The high technical standards of the country are also seen in the harnessing of energy (whether by water, coal, oil, or natural gas), as also in the opening up of access to the rich mineral resources in the ground.

STATES OF THE UNITED STATES

State	Area sq. mi.	Area sq. km.	Population (1970 census)
Alabama	50,708	131,333	3,444,165
Alaska	566,432	1,467,052	302,173
Arizona	113,417	293,749	1,772,482
Arkansas	51,945	134,537	1,923,295
California	156,361	404,973	19,953,134
Colorado	103,766	268,753	2,207,259
Connecticut	4,862	12,593	3,032,217
Delaware	1,982	5,133	548,104
Florida	54,090	140,092	6,789,443
Georgia	58,073	150,408	4,589,575
Hawaii	6,425	16,641	769,913
Idaho	82,677	214,132	713,008
Illinois	55,748	144,387	11,113,976
Indiana	36,097	93,491	5,193,669
Iowa	55,941	144,887	2,825,041
Kansas	81,787	211,827	2,249,071
Kentucky	39,650	102,693	3,219,311
Louisiana	44,930	116,368	3,643,180
Maine	30,920	80,082	993,663
Maryland	9,891	25,618	3,922,399
Massachusetts	7,826	20,269	5,689,170
Michigan	56,817	147,155	8,875,083
Minnesota	79,289	205,358	3,805,069
Mississippi	47,296	122,496	2,216,912
Missouri	68,995	178,696	4,677,399
Montana	145,587	377,069	694,409
Nebraska	76,483	198,090	1,483,791
Nevada	109,889	284,611	488,738
New Hampshire	9,027	23,380	737,681
New Jersey	7,521	19,479	7,168,164
New Mexico	121,412	314,457	1,016,000
New York	47,831	123,882	18,241,266
North Carolina	48,798	126,386	5,082,059
North Dakota	69,273	179,416	617,761
Ohio	40,975	106,125	10,652,017
Oklahoma	68,782	178,145	2,559,253
Oregon	96,184	249,115	2,091,385
Pennsylvania	44,966	116,461	11,793,909
Rhode Island	1,049	2,717	949,723
South Carolina	30,225	78,282	2,590,516
South Dakota	75,955	196,723	666,257
Tennessee	41,328	107,039	3,924,164
Texas	262,134	678,924	11,196,730
Utah	82,096	212,628	1,059,273
Vermont	9,276	24,025	444,732
Virginia	39,780	103,030	4,648,494
Washington	66,570	172,416	3,409,169
West Virginia	24,070	62,341	1,744,237
Wisconsin	54,464	141,061	4,417,933
Wyoming	97,203	251,755	332,416

Right: The Panama Canal cuts through Central America to connect the Atlantic and Pacific oceans. By the construction of this canal at the narrowest point of the land bridge between North and South America, ships have been spared the time-wasting circumnavigation of the South American continent. A superb feat of engineering, the canal, which was built by the United States in the early 1900s, is 50.7 miles (81.6 km) long.

Right: Temple of the Warriors in the ancient Maya city of Chichén Itzá, in Mexico. Many such eloquent witnesses to Maya culture, which was at its height from the AD 300s to 600s, were for centuries buried in deep and lonely forestland. It was not until the 19th century that the magnificent relics of the old Maya towns were rediscovered.

SOUTH AMERICA

BRAZIL/ARGENTINA—The Iguaçu Falls, part of the border between Brazil and Argentina

South America has an area of nearly 7 million square miles (18 million sq km). Some of the typical characteristics of North America are reproduced there. Like the more northerly continent, South America is also traversed from north to south along the Pacific coast by a continuous and mighty chain of high mountains. With their length of 4,500 miles (7,250 km), the Andes of South America are the longest mountain chain in the world. Their highest point is Mount Aconcagua, in Argentina, which is almost 23,000 feet (7,000 metres) high. On the other coast there is a highland region made up of the Guiana Highlands and the Brazilian Highlands. And as in North America, there are extensive lowlands between the western Andes and the eastern highlands. Enormous parts of northern South America are covered by impenetrable tropical primeval forest. Huge herds of cattle graze on the Argentinian steppes, the Pampas. In the south, the land then merges into the desert-like steppes of Patagonia.

South America has particularly mighty rivers. The sources of the Amazon rise in the west, in the Peruvian Andes. As this river receives one tributary after another, it becomes the river with the greatest flow of water on the continent, finally flowing through Brazil to its mouth in the Atlantic Ocean. With its course of nearly 4,000 miles (6,500 km), it is the second longest river in the world, and its delta, some 155 miles (250 km) wide, is the largest in the world. Together with its tributaries, it flows through the apparently endless 'Green Hell' of hot and humid rain forests. Exploration here is extremely dangerous, but a motorway is now being constructed through the jungle.

After the discovery of the Americas, attempts were quickly made to open up the interior of the southern continent. Scarcely had the great sea-dogs taken the news of their explorations back to Europe, than Spanish conquistadors and Portuguese adventurers went out in search of gold and fabulous wealth. This was followed by the foundation, on the part of the Spaniards and Portuguese, of great colonial territories in South America, and these gave to the continent a stamp that it has never lost. The influence of these European nations can still be found all over, particularly in the languages. Portuguese is spoken in Brazil, and Spanish in all the other countries. Furthermore, throughout the whole of South America, the Roman Catholic religion occupies a dominant position.

South America has abundant natural wealth, but it has many difficult problems in the economic field. On the one hand, there is a rich minority, which owns nearly all the land, and on the other, there are great masses of impoverished smallholders, agricultural labourers, and South American Indians. There is a general tendency to migrate to the towns, and this leads to unemployment, because industrialization has not yet been adequately accomplished. Lack of work forces the poorest of all to build themselves shanty towns on the outskirts of the cities—a striking contrast to the modern luxury buildings and the heavy motor traffic.

New ideas designed to improve living standards are slow to be implemented. A regular system of education is usually found only in the towns. In most countries, the position of the government is weak, because the military, being the force of law and order, wields too much power. As a result, uprisings and revolutions in South America are commonplace. But although the social difficulties are enormous, one of the great problems of North America has been spared the southern continent. For centuries in South America, Whites, South American Indians, and Negroes have mixed together, so that racial problems are comparatively minor.

ARGENTINA Area 1,073,000 sq miles (2,779,000 sq km); population 23,360,000; capital, Buenos Aires (pop. 8,353,000); currency, peso (100 centavos); official language, Spanish.

Argentina has been independent since 1816, and a federal republic since 1853. The country is 2,300 miles (3,700 km) long from north to south, almost half the length of the continent. In the north-west, there is the hot bush and forest lowland of the Gran Chaco, to the south the steppe lowlands of the Pampas, which extend as far as the coast, and in the west the Andes, which contain the highest mountain in South America, the 22,835 feet (6,960 metres) high Aconçagua. The climate varies from almost tropical in the Gran Chaco to cool in the south. In the damp north-eastern marginal areas, there is tropical primeval forest, in which palms, lianas, bamboo, mimosa, and acacia grow.

Ninety per cent of Argentinians are white, mostly of Spanish or Italian descent. A small German minority, however, wields considerable economic influence. Some pure-blooded Amerindians live in the Gran Chaco.

The basis of the economy is agriculture, but huge herds of cattle graze on the Pampas, and beef is an important export. The Pampas merge into a crescent-shaped region, nearly 200 miles (320 km) broad, in which grain is cultivated. Cotton is planted in the Gran Chaco, and the province of Tucumán in the north-west is a sugar-cane growing region. The mountains have considerable mineral resources, but these are largely undeveloped.

BOLIVIA Area 415,000 sq miles (1,075,000 sq km); population 4,658,000; capital, La Paz (pop. 553,000); currency, peso (100 centavos); official language, Spanish.

Under the leadership of Simón Bolívar, from which it took its name, the country declared its independence from Spain and Peru in 1825.

Bolivia is completely landlocked. In the west, ranges of the Andes (the Cordilleras), with peaks rising to 20,000 feet (6,100 metres), border the Altiplano, a treeless plateau some 12,500 feet (3,800 metres) above sea level. Here, in an elevated basin, lies Lake Titicaca. The eastern lowlands have affinities with the grass steppes (llanos) of the Amazon Basin and with the Gran Chaco, and they are sparsely populated. More than half the people live in the Altiplano, particularly on the slopes falling away to the east. Only 15 per cent are Whites, but they constitute the ruling class. More than half are Indians, and the rest are of mixed blood, mostly Mestizos. Two-thirds of the population, especially the South American Indians, are engaged in agriculture, but their primitive methods produce poor results, although the llanos are very fertile. The land has considerable mineral resources, especially of tin, but these are yet to be fully exploited.

BRAZIL Area 3,286,488 sq miles (8,511,964 sq km); population 93,000,000; capital, Brasília (pop. 545,000); currency, cruzeiro (100 centavos); official language, Portuguese.

Brazil declared its independence from Portugal in 1822, and became a republic in 1889. It is the fifth largest country in the world, taking up almost half the South American continent. The main river is the Amazon, in the north, with some hundred navigable tributaries. The Amazon lowlands have a hot and humid climate and constitute the largest tropical primeval forest region in the world. To the north lie the largely unexplored Guiana Highlands, which are partly covered with primeval forest, partly with savanna vegetation. Rain forests lie along the central coastal regions, while in the south-east there are subtropical forests and savanna. Savanna also dominate extensive regions of the highlands in the interior.

Brazil has a larger population than any other South American country. Until the mid-1600s, there was considerable immigration of Portuguese and Spaniards, and from the end of the 1500s Negro slaves were brought into the country. It was not until the 19th century that free immigration began from all the countries of Europe. Today, barely 60 per cent of the inhabitants are White. There are small groups of Negroes and Japanese, but a third are Mestizos and Zambos. And there are nearly 100,000 Amerindians, principally in the Amazon region.

Brazil's wealth comes from agriculture. More than half of the whole work force is engaged in agriculture and forestry. The main crop is coffee. The country also has rich mineral resources, and industrialization is being actively promoted.

CHILE Area 292,000 sq miles (756,000 sq km); population 10,000,000; capital, Santiago (pop. 4,000,000); currency, escudo (100 centésimos); official language, Spanish.

A former Spanish colony, Chile has been independent since 1818. It is a long, mountainous country, stretching along the Pacific coast for more than half the length of South America. There are three distinct climatic zones: in the north, a dry, desert zone with a rainless coast; in the centre, a subtropical zone; and in the south, a zone with heavy rainfall and low summer temperatures.

Between the Andes—the High Cordilleras in the east and the Coastal Cordilleras in the west—runs a great longitudinal valley. There are earthquake zones, and active volcanoes rising to a height of 22,000 feet (6,700 metres). Tierra del Fuego, the southern tip of the continent, is separated from the mainland by the stormy Strait of Magellan.

Most of the population are Mestizos. Of the original Indian native population, only about 500,000 are left. The small ruling class comes from people of European descent. Almost three-quarters of the inhabitants live in the central area, for this is the only part of the country that is arable. Extensive regions require artificial irrigation. There are rich mineral resources, and of all exported products, 80 per cent are mined (copper, iron, nitrates).

COLOMBIA Area 439,737 sq miles (1,138,914 sq km); population 22,000,000; capital, Bogotá (pop. 2,512,000); currency, peso (100 centavos); official language, Spanish.

Colombia won independence from Spain in 1819, and became a republic in 1886. It lies in the north-west of South America, bordering on Panama, which, for some time, formed part of Colombia. The Eastern Cordilleras, a range of the Andes, reach a height of 18,000 feet (5,500 metres). The lowlands of the Amazon valley and the Orinoco occupy large portions of the country, on both the Pacific and Caribbean coasts.

More than two-thirds of the population are Mestizos, a fifth are Whites, and the rest are Negroes, Mslattoes, and Zambos. The original Indian population is today represented by only about 2 per cent of the inhabitants.

Although Colombia is developing its industry, it is still largely an agricultural country. Very little of the land is under cultivation.

BRAZIL—Rio de Janeiro

BRAZIL—Native hut in primeval Amazon forest

PERU—Old Inca village

BRAZIL—National Congress Buildings, Brasília

Left: The tropical rain forests of the Amazon region in South America cover an area of about a million square miles (2.5 million sq km). The vegetation is so dense that the light of day never reaches the ground. In the morning, hot air rises continually and clouds form in which electric storms build up. When the midday heat has passed its peak, torrents of rain water descend—in quantities that during a single day are equivalent to the precipitation of a whole year for, say, Rome or Paris.

Left: Angel Falls, the highest waterfall in the world. The falls thunder down from a height of 3,212 feet (979 metres) in the Guiana Highlands of Venezuela.

Below: An American Indian makes fire by rubbing two sticks together. In the primeval forest of South America, there are still primitive, almost unknown American Indian tribes. The white people live only in the few townships along the giant rivers.

There are large numbers of smallholders. The main product is coffee.

ECUADOR *Area 109,500 sq miles (283,600 sq km); population 7,000,000; capital Quito (pop. 700,000); currency, sucre (100 centavos); official language, Spanish.*

Ecuador has been an independent republic since 1830. It suffers from constant uprisings, revolutions, and putsches, under which the country's economic development has been retarded. As a result, it is amongst the poorest countries of South America. It lies on the west coast of the continent, between Peru and Colombia. The coastal lowlands are from 30 to 90 miles (50-150 km) wide. Through the centre of the country run two parallel mountain chains of the Andes, with heights of 10,000-20,000 feet (3,000-6,000 metres). There are large numbers of active volcanoes in this region. Towards the east, the mountain slopes fall steeply away down to the lowlands of the Amazon valley.

Over a third of the inhabitants are Amerindians, engaged in agriculture. The coastal region is inhabited by Mestizos, Negroes, and Mulattoes. The 10 per cent of Whites, chiefly descendants of the Spaniards, constitute the ruling class. Two-thirds of the population are engaged in agriculture or cattle rearing.

FRENCH GUIANA *Area 34,740 sq miles (89,976 sq km); population, 48,000; capital, Cayenne (pop. 20,000); currency, franc (French); official language, French.*

The country, which lies on the northern coast of South America, became an overseas department of France in 1946. Most of the people are Negroes or Creoles, and about 10 per cent are American Indians. Tropical rain forest covers almost nine-tenths of the total area, and is still unexplored. Gold is mined and there are large deposits of bauxite. Crops grown include sugar and maize.

GUYANA *Area 83,000 sq miles (215,000 sq km); population 714,000; capital, Georgetown*

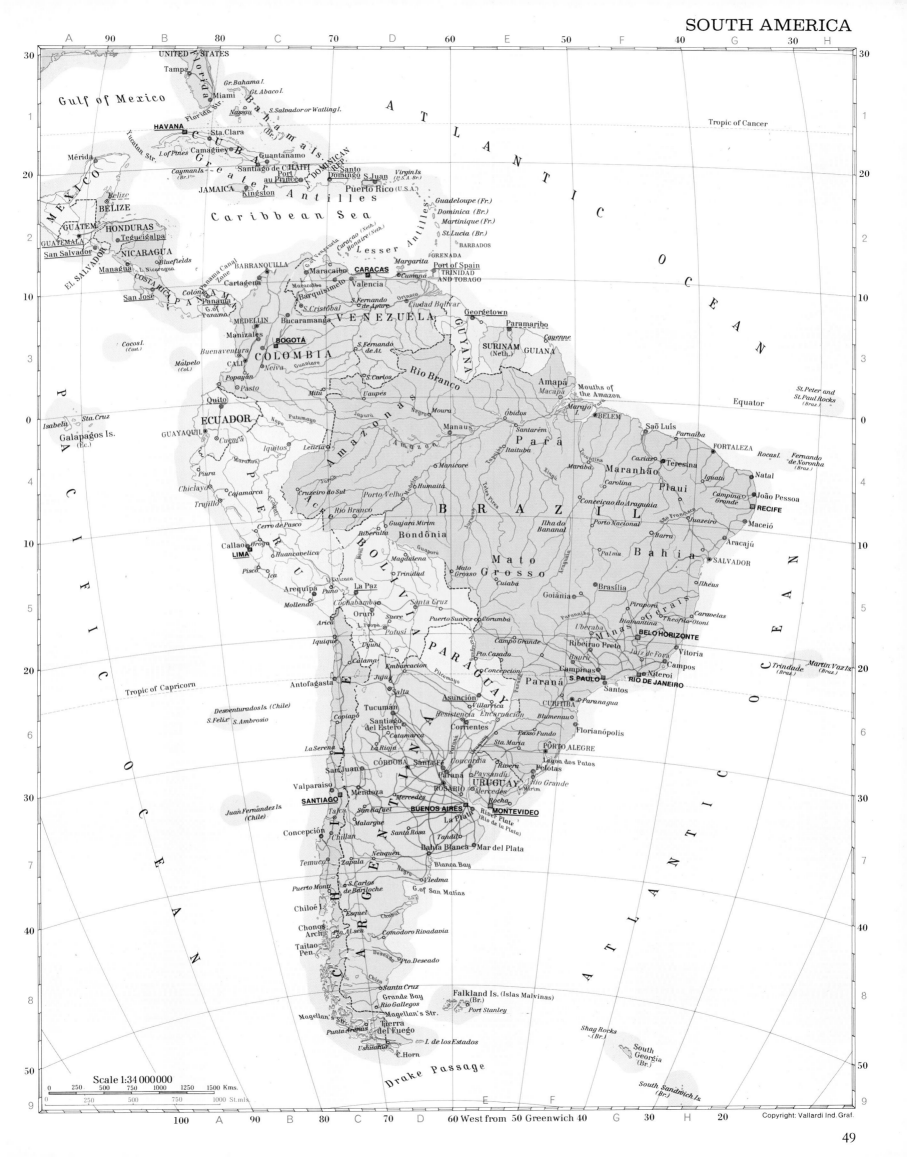

A 90 B 80 C 70 D 60 E 50 F 40 G 30 H

Gulf of Mexico

UNITED STATES
Tampa
Miami
Gr. Bahama I.
Gt. Abaco I.
Florida Str. Nassau
S. Salvador or Watling I.
Bahama Is.
HAVANA □ CUBA Sta. Clara
Mérida
Yucatan Str. *I. of Pines* Camagüey Guantánamo
Caymans Is. Santiago de CHAITI DOMINICAN
(Br.) Port REP.
MEXICO au Prince Santo S. Juan *Virgin Is.*
JAMAICA Domingo Puerto Rico (U.S.A.) (U.S.A. Br.)
Kingston

ATLANTIC

Tropic of Cancer

BELIZE
Belize
GUATEM. HONDURAS
GUATEMALA Tegucigalpa
San Salvador NICARAGUA
EL SALVADOR Managua *Bluefields*
L. Nicaragua
San José COSTA RICA
Colón PANAMA
PANAMA
G. of Panama

Puerto Rico (U.S.A.)
Guadeloupe (Fr.)
Dominica (Br.)
Martinique (Fr.)
St. Lucia (Br.)
BARBADOS
GRENADA
Port of Spain
TRINIDAD
AND TOBAGO

Caribbean Sea

Lesser Antilles

Curaçao (Neth.)
Bonaire (Neth.)
BARRANQUILLA *G. of Venezuela*
Cartagena Maracaibo CARACAS
Barquisimeto Valencia Cumaná
Maracaibo Orinoco
S. Cristóbal S. Fernando Margarita
MEDELLIN Bucaramanga de Apure Ciudad Bolívar Georgetown
Manizales VENEZUELA Paramaribo
Buenaventura BOGOTÁ Cayenne
Málpelo CALI S. Fernando GUYANA SURINAM
(Col.) COLOMBIA de At. (Neth.) GUIANA
Popayán Neiva *Guaviare* Amapá
Pasto Río Branco Macapá Mouths of
Quito Mitú *Uaupés* the Amazon

O C E A N

St. Peter and
St. Paul Rocks
(Braz.)

Equator

ECUADOR
GUAYAQUIL Cuenca *Napo* Moura
Morona Iquitos *Putumayo* Manaus Óbidos Marajó I. BELEM
Piura Leticia Santarém São Luís Parnaíba Rocas I. Fernando
Japurá Pará FORTALEZA de Noronha
Chiclayo Cajamarca *Amazon* *Juruá* Itaituba Carias Teresina (Braz.)
Trujillo *Marañon* Manicore Maranhão Iguatú Natal
Cruzeiro do Sul *Madeira* Humaitá *Tapajós* *Maraba* Piauí João Pessoa
Acre Río Branco Porto Velho *Xingu* Carolina *São Francisco* Campina RECIFE
Cerro de Pasco Conceição do Araguaia Grande
Callao Oroya BRAZIL Porto Nacional Juazeiro Maceió
LIMA Huancavelica Guajará Mirim Ilha do *Tocantins* Barra Aracajú
Riberalta Rondônia Bananal Bahia
Pisco Ica Magdalena Mato Palma SALVADOR
Arequipa Puno BOLIVIA Trinidad Grosso Ilhéus
Mollendo Cochabamba *Guaporé* Cuiabá
Arica La Paz Santa Cruz Goiânia Brasília Piraporá Caravelas
Oruro Sucre Puerto Suárez Corumbá *Gerais* Diamantina Theofilo Otoni
L. Poopó Potosí Paranaíba Uberaba Minas
Iquique Campo Grande Ribeirão Preto BELO HORIZONTE
PARAGUAY Bauru Vitória
CHILE Calama Embarcación Concepción *Paraná* Campinas Campos
Antofagasta Jujuy Pto. Casado Paraná Niteroi
Uyuni Pilcomayo S. PAULO RIO DE JANEIRO
Tropic of Capricorn Salta Asunción Santos
Desventurados Is. (Chile) Copiapó Tucumán Villarrica Encarnación CURITIBA Paranaguá
S. Felix S. Ambrosio Santiago Resistencia Blumenau
del Estero Corrientes Passo Florianópolis
La Serena Catamarca ARGENTINA Sta. Maria Fundo PÔRTO ALEGRE
San Juan La Rioja *Paraná* Concordia Rivera Lagôa dos Patos
Valparaíso CÓRDOBA Santa Fé Paysandú Pelotas
SANTIAGO Mendoza Rosario URUGUAY Rio Grande
Talca Paraná Mercedes Río Negro
San Rafael Mercedes MONTEVIDEO Rocha
Malargue BUENOS AIRES L. Mirim
Concepción La Plata River Plate
Chillán Santa Rosa (Río de la Plata)
Temuco Zapala Neuquén Bahía Blanca Mar del Plata
Negro Blanca Bay
Puerto Montt S. Carlos Viedma
de Bariloche G. of San Matías
Chiloé I.
Esquel *Chubut*
Chonos Comodoro Rivadavia
Arch. ARGENTINA
Taitao *Deseado* Pto. Deseado
Pen. *Chico*
Santa Cruz Falkland Is. (Islas Malvinas)
Grande Bay (Br.)
Río Gallegos Port Stanley
Magellan's Str. Shag Rocks
Punta Arenas Magellan's Str. (Br.) South
Tierra I. de los Estados Georgia
del Fuego (Br.)
C. Horn
Ushuaia South Sandwich Is.
(Br.)

Drake Passage

PACIFIC OCEAN

ATLANTIC OCEAN

Galapagos Is.
(Ec.)
Isabela Sta. Cruz

Cocos I.
(Cost.)

Trindade
(Braz.)
Martin Vaz Is
(Braz.)

Juan Fernández Is.
(Chile)

Scale 1:34 000 000
0 250 750 1250 1500 Kms.
500 1000
0 250 500 750 1000 St. mls.

100 A 90 B 80 C 70 D 60 West from 50 Greenwich 40 G 30 H 20

(pop. 168,000); currency, dollar (100 cents); official language, English.

Formerly British Guiana, the country became an independent member of the Commonwealth in 1966, the world's first Co-operative Republic. Guyana lies between Venezuela and Surinam on the Atlantic Ocean. The highland region in the west rises to a height of nearly 10,000 feet (3,000 metres). The mountains in the east are much flatter and give way to tropical rain forests. Most of the population live on the coastal strip. About half of them are Indians (whose ancestors came from India). The Whites and the American Ind ans constitute only a small group. There are, however, large numbers of Negroes and Mulattoes. Bauxite, aluminium oxide, manganese ores, and diamonds are mined and exported. Sugar, rice, and rum are also exported.

NETHERLANDS ANTILLES *Area 383 sq miles (993 sq km); population 224,000; capital, Willemstad (pop. 146,000); currency, guilder (Dutch); official language, Dutch.*

These islands, also known as the Dutch West Indies, have independence of administration and enjoy equal rights with the Netherlands themselves. They consist of Aruba, Bonaire, and Curaçao off the Venezuelan coast, and three smaller islands of the Windward group. The inhabitants are principally Negroes and Mulattoes. The economy is based on the refining of oil imported from Venezuela to Aruba and Curaçao.

PARAGUAY *Area 157,000 sq miles (406,600 sq km); population 2,314,000; capital, Asunción (pop. 437,000); currency, guaraní (100 céntimos); official language, Spanish.*

Paraguay won its independence from Spain and became a republic in 1811. The larger, western part of the country lies in the Gran Chaco, whereas the eastern part is bordered by the Paraná and constitutes an undulating tableland with subtropical rain forests. Between the Paraguay and Paraná rivers, there are large marshes. Some 95 per cent of the inhabitants are Mestizos. More than half the people live in or around the capital. And more than half are engaged in agriculture.

PERU *Area 496,000 sq miles (1,285,000 sq km); population 14,000,000; capital, Lima (pop. 3,600,000); currency, sol (100 centavos); official language, Spanish.*

Peru declared its independence from Spain in 1821, and after many internal political troubles eventually became a republic. It has a 1,400-mile (2,250-km) coastal strip on the Pacific Ocean, which is fertile only along the river banks. The country is traversed from north to south by the Cordilleras (Andes), the highest peak being Huascarán, at 22,205 feet (6,768 metres). The eastern chain of the Cordilleras merges into the highland region of the Montana, and this, in turn, gives way to wooded lowlands. The main sources of the Amazon rise in the Peruvian Andes.

Most of the inhabitants are descended from American Indians, but the Whites constitute the ruling class. Quechua and Aymara, American Indian languages, are widely spoken. Half of the working population are engaged in agriculture, forestry, and fishing. On the large arable areas of the coastal district, cotton, sugar-cane, rice, maize, and many other crops are grown on plantations. There are extensive irrigation systems. There is also a flourishing mining industry.

SURINAM *Area 63,000 sq miles (163,000 sq*

Above: The wide-open spaces of the Bolivian highlands are dry and cold, and extensively covered with thorn-bushes. The American Indians living there rear alpacas and llamas, animals related to the camel. Their excellent wool is highly prized, and they are also good beasts of burden.

Centre: Machu Picchu, Peru. When the first White men visited Peru in the early 1500s, there were American Indians living between Peru and Bolivia, who were ruled by the Incas. Their mighty king was considered to be the son of the sun-god and was correspondingly revered. The Incas had a rigid political and religious organization, with a system of class distinction according to which each had his own special place. There were strict laws governing the way in which public works, including terracing and irrigation, had to be carried out. Qualified engineers built roads, bridges, and towns. One of the most impressive of the towns was Machu Picchu. Its situation between two mighty mountain peaks was of great importance. It provided an ideal site for a temple, a place of sacrifice, a solar observatory, and houses for 10,000 people, all built on successive terraces. Even agriculture was carried out on terraces specially laid out for the purpose. A road with a hard surface made communication with the capital city easier.

Left: South American Indians in their traditional balsa-wood boats, fishing on Lake Titicaca. This is the second largest lake in South America, and straddles the border between Peru and Bolivia. Lying in a basin in the Andes, it is higher than any other large navigable body of water in the world, standing 12,507 feet (3,812 metres) above sea level.

km); population 480,000; capital, Paramaribo (pop. 110,000); currency, guilder (100 cents); official language, Dutch.

Surinam, also known as Dutch Guiana, is an autonomous unit of the Netherlands. It lies on the northern coast of South America. Three-quarters of the land area is covered in forest, still largely unexplored. Half the inhabitants are of mixed blood. Along the coast, sugar-cane, coffee, citrus fruits, and cacao are cultivated, and there are vast deposits of bauxite.

TRINIDAD AND TOBAGO Area 1,980 sq miles (5,130 sq km); population 1,010,000; capital, Port of Spain (pop. 94,000); currency, dollar (100 cents); official language, English.

These two islands, the most southerly of the Lesser Antilles, formed a British colony from 1889 until their independence in 1962. They lie off the coast of Venezuela. The population of Tobago, by far the smaller of the two islands, consists almost exclusively of Negroes. On Trinidad, more than a third of the people are Indians, but the majority are Negroes or Mulattoes. Trinidad is a mountainous island and has large stretches of rain forest. Half of the country is cultivated (sugar and cocoa), and there are rich deposits of oil and natural asphalt.

URUGUAY Area 68,536 sq miles (177,507 sq km); population 2,500,000; capital, Montevideo (pop. 1,173,000); currency, peso (100 centésimos); official language, Spanish.

Uruguay became an independent republic in 1828, having belonged first to Spain and then to Brazil. It is situated on the Atlantic Ocean and on the Río de la Plata, between Brazil and Argentina. Hilly grassland merges in the south into the Argentinian Pampas. The population consists largely of the descendants of Spanish and Portuguese settlers. The main source of income is the rearing of animals. Meat, meat products, and wool are exported. More than two-thirds of the total area is pastureland, only 10 per cent being arable.

VENEZUELA Area 352,145 sq miles (912,051 sq km); population 10,722,000; capital, Caracas (pop. 2,184,000); currency, bolívar (100 céntimos); official language, Spanish.

Venezuela won its independence from Spain in 1821 and became a republic in 1830. It lies in the northernmost part of South America, between Colombia and Guyana. The main river is the Orinoco, which drains four-fifths of the country. Mountain systems break up Venezuela into four distinct regions: the Maracaibo lowlands, the highlands in the north and north-west, the vast Orinoco plains or *llanos*, and the Guiana Highlands. The llanos, in the south-east, cover a third of the country's area.

The population consists mainly of 65 per cent Mestizos, 20 per cent Whites, and 10 per cent Negroes. Only 1 per cent are pure-blooded South American Indians. Half of the inhabitants live in the towns.

For years, agriculture was the only source of revenue, with exports of coffee and cocoa. Now, however, Venezuela has developed into an important supplier of raw materials for industry. It is the fifth largest oil-producing country in the world, and the largest exporter. Its oil resources are found mainly in the Maracaibo basin. Its iron ore deposits are also among the largest in the world, and there are important gold and diamond mines. Along with the development of refineries, the country is also being increasingly industrialized.

Above: A herd of cattle in southern Chile. Chile is a narrow country with a long coast on the Pacific Ocean. As a result of its great length, its climate and geographical features vary considerably. The extremely wet southern part has many lakes, and large tracts of land are used for pasture.

Right: A South American gaucho, cowboy of the pampas. Brazil, Paraguay, and Argentina are largely pampas land, steppe land covering an area of some 1½ million square miles (4 million sq. km). It is widely believed that the stock of animals on these pasturelands goes back to a single bull and seven cows that ran away from a Portuguese settler in 1522 while he was landing his possessions on the Río de la Plata. This is the kingdom of the gauchos, who have the reputation of being particularly brave. They certainly have to be very skilful when lassoing the animals, a feat often accompanied by equestrian arts of a high and, sometimes, unusual order.

In contrast to most South American countries, Argentina has good roads and railways. Great demands were made on the ingenuity of the engineers responsible for building railways over the Andes, a formidable mountain range abounding in raging torrents and deep crevices. These demands were adequately met in practice. Today, two trans-Andean railway lines link Argentina with Chile, and are among the highest railways in the world. The older of the two lines *(right)*, the one between Mendoza and Santiago, was commissioned in 1904.

OCEANIA

POLYNESIA—Aerial view of one of the countless Pacific atolls

Oceania consists of the continent of Australia and a number of islands and atolls, distributed over the vast spaces of the Pacific Ocean. With its area of some 3 million square miles (nearly 8 million sq km), Australia alone occupies seven-eighths of the land mass of Oceania. Australia is the smallest of the earth's continents and, at the same time, the most sparsely populated. Its population density is just over 4 persons to the sq mile (nearly 2/sq km), whereas the figures for England are 916 per square mile (354/sq km). The total population of Oceania is estimated at 20 millions, i.e. about a third of the population of Great Britain. Some geographers do not include Austhalia and some other large islands in Oceania, but use the term to define the three large groups of Pacific Islands—Melanesia, Micronesia, and Polynesia.

Soon after America had been discovered, the Europeans began to interest themselves in this faraway corner of the world. The Portuguese seafarer Ferdinand Magellan, who was in the service of the Spanish king, was the first to land on the Marianas in 1521, as he was making the first circum-navigation of the globe. The discovery and settlement of Australia came about in rather a haphazard way. The country was first sighted by a Spaniard, Luis Vaes de Torres, at the beginning of the 17th century, but he confined himself to sailing along a portion of the northern coastline. Then, a Dutchman, Abel Tasman, anchored his ship in 1642 in a friendly bay of a land he called Van Diemen's Land, and took possession of it in the name of his country. This land turned out to be an island, however, later to be called Tasmania after him. He also discovered New Zealand on this voyage, but had unwittingly sailed right round Australia without sighting it. On his next voyage, in 1644, Tasman explored the northern coast of the mysterious 'South Land' (Australia), finding it a bleak and hostile land, and Dutch exploration around Australian waters virtually ended with Tasman. Thus, the true and final discovery of the continent can be attributed to the great English sea-rover Captain James Cook, over 100 years later. In 1769, sailing from Tahiti, he first charted the New Zealand coast in detail and then, in 1770, became the first European to see the eastern coast of Australia (then known as New Holland). He made his famous landing at Botany Bay on April 29, and claimed the land for his country. On a second voyage of exploration (1772-75), Cook visited Easter Island, the Marquesas, the Society Islands, Niue, Tonga, the New Hebrides, New Caledonia, and Norfolk Island. In 1787, the British government deported 717 convicts, men and women, most of whom had been found guilty of minor misdemeanours. They established a settlement at Sydney on 26 January 1788. The lot of these convicts in Australia was not quite so dreadful as it might have seemed to many at the time. The land that was to be their prison proved in many respects to be exceedingly fertile, and the lawbreakers became farmers. Later, standard varieties of grain and animals were imported to Australia for the benefit of the Europeans, and sheep and cattle became the continent's wealth.

Today, Australia and New Zealand are peopled by inhabitants of varied origins, but they are mostly Whites, immigrants or the descendants of immigrants. In the Pacific islands, however, the native populations are predominant. The three large groups of islands each cover enormous areas of the Pacific, and the groupings are based partly on the types of islands and partly on the people who live on them. Roughly, Melanesia covers the south-west Pacific, Micronesia the north-west, and Polynesia all the islands east of the International Date Line (and a few west of it).

AUSTRALIA *Area 2,967,909 sq miles (7,686,848 sq km); population 13,091,000; capital, Canberra (pop. 165,000); currency, dollar (100 cents); official language, English.*

The Australian Commonwealth was founded in 1901, comprising Nlw South Wales, Victoria, Queensland, South Australia, Western Australia, and Tasmania. The Northern Territory was transferred from South Australia 10 years later, at the same time as the Australian Capital Territory was acquired from New South Wales. Australia is a member of the British Commonwealth, and a parliamentary democracy. The head of state is the British monarch, represented by a governor-general, who formally appoints the prime minister and other ministers from the majority party in parliament. Parliament (the House of Representatives and the Senate) is the legislative body.

Australia is the smallest of the continents, although it may also be regarded as the largest island in the world. The area of the mainland (i.e. without Tasmania) is 2,941,526 square miles (7,618,517 sq km), and it has a coastline of over 11,000 square miles (28,500 sq km). The eastern and more populated part of the country has a regular coastline, with good harbours and rivers flowing to the sea. The western half has a broken coastline and estuaries rather than rivers. The Great Barrier Reef, the largest coral reef in the world, stretches for about 1,250 miles (2,000 km) parallel to the Queensland coast at a distance of 10-150 miles (15-240 km). It covers an area of some 80,000 sq miles (200,000 sq km). Much of Australia's interior, especially in the west, is desert. But in the east, particularly the south-east, and in most of the coastal areas, the land is fertile.

The country as a whole is generally low and flat, but there are highlands stretching right along the east coast and along most of Victoria on the southern coast, the highest point being Mount Kosciusko, which rises 7,316 feet (2,230 metres) in the Australian Alps, near Canberra. In the centre of the continent, lowlands extend from the Gulf of Carpentaria to the shores of the Great Australian Bight in the south. A vast plateau, with an average height of about 1,000 feet (300 metres), covers most of the western two-thirds of Australia. A largely desert region, it includes Western Australia, the Northern Territory, and much of South Australia, extending even into Queensland and New South Wales.

Australia has a warm, dry climate, the northern third of the country lying in the tropics. Only about a third of the country receives enough rain for good farming. Nevertheless, what good pastureland and arable land there is makes Australia the leading wool producing nation in the world and one of the leading meat and wheat exporting countries. Most of the farms are family concerns covering large areas and run with the help of machinery and seasonal workers. In the Northern Territory, some ranches, or *stations* as they are called, cover several thousand square miles.

But Australia is not just an agricultural and farming country. Mining is becoming increasingly important. The gold deposits have long been known, but rich strata of iron ore have also been discovered, and Australia leads the world in the production of lead. Other important minerals include hard and brown coal, bauxite, copper, and zinc. There are several oilfields in production (in Queensland, Western Australia, and offshore Victoria), which supply about two-thirds of the country's needs. Natural gas deposits are also being exploited. Industry has grown enormously, but there is a shortage of manpower to develop all the possibilities offered by this vast country. Economists believe that Australia could support three times its present population.

Most of the inhabitants of Australia are European immigrants or descendants of immigrants. Only about 100,000 of the original native race, the Aborigines, remain, and most of these live on protected reserves. They used to wander through the country beachcombing and hunting. They used primitive implements and weapons (spears, clubs, boomerangs) made of bone, sea-shells, rock, or wood. The Aborigines have chocolate-brown skin and certain physical characteristics that do not place them easily into any of the major racial stocks. They probably lived originally in south-eastern Asia.

The native animal world of Australia is markedly different from that found in other countries of the world, and this phenomenon can be explained by the development undergone by the earth's crust. Some 200 million years ago, the great land mass that existed then broke up. As it broke away, each continent naturally carried with it the varieties of animal that lived there. These then developed in isolation from the others. So it is that only in Australia do we find the duckbilled platypus and the spiny anteater (echidna), representing a primitive subspecies of mammals. These lay eggs, hatch them out, and then feed their young on breast milk. A special variety of mammal is also found in Australia, the marsupials. These give birth to living young, which are so small that they slip into the mother's pouch immediately after birth. There they are suckled until they are large enough to live an independent life. The best known of these is the kangaroo, but there are also koalas, wombats, bandicoots, dasyures, Tasmanian wolves, and the ape-like cuscus.

FIJI *Area 7,055 sq miles (18,272 sq km); population 541,000; capital, Suva (pop. 54,000); currency, dollar (100 cents); official language, English.*

A group of 322 islands in the South Pacific, some 1,100 miles (1,770 km) north of New Zealand, Fiji came under British control in 1874 and became an independent nation within the Commonwealth in 1970. Only 106 of the islands are inhabited, and the largest two, Viti Levu and Vanua Levu, make up seven-eighths of the total area. About half the people are Indians and some 42 per cent are Fijians. The Indians are largely descended from plantation labourers brought from India between 1880 and 1914. The islands have a favourable oceanic climate, and the main agricultural products are sugar-cane and coconuts. Tourism is becoming an increasingly important source of revenue.

FRENCH POLYNESIA *Area 1,550 sq miles (4,000 sq km); population 120,000; capital, Papeete (pop. 15,000).*

An Overseas Territory of France since 1958, French Polynesia consists of a number of islands scattered over a wide area of the eastern Pacific. These include the Society Islands, the Leeward Isles, and the Marquesas. The capital is located on Tahiti, in the Society group. Most of the people are Polynesians. The most important product is copra.

GILBERT & ELLICE ISLANDS *Area 324 sq miles (839 sq km); population 58,000; capital,*

AUSTRALIA—Ayers Rock, 1,100 feet (335 metres) high

AUSTRALIA—The spectacular Sydney Harbour Bridge

AUSTRALIA—The Macdonnell Ranges in central Australia
POLYNESIA—Easter Island, with its enigmatic statues

1

NORTH
AMERICA

G. of California
Lower California

Guadalupe I.

Cedros I.

C. St. Lucas

7060

Hawaiian Islands

re I.
Midway Is.

Lisianski I.   Laysan I.
Maro Reef   Gardner
Pinnacles

Tropic of Cancer   3767

Revilla Gigedo
Is.

Necker I.

Necker   Nihoa   Kauai
Ridge   Niihau   Oahu   Honolulu
Lanai   Maui
4213   Mauna Kea
Hawaii

983

833

Johnston I.

F   P   A   C   I   F   I   C

901

O

Palmyra I.
Washington I.
Fanning I.

3092

436

C   E

Christmas I.

Howland I.   7251
Baker I.

Jarvis I.

Equator

Phoenix Is.
Canton I.   7375
Phoenix I.
Gardner I.   Hull I.   Sydney I.   2204

Malden I.

A

Starbuck I.

Filippo Reef

Atafu
Fakaofo
Tokelau Is.
(Union Group)

Pukapuka Atoll
(Danger Is.)

Penrhyn A.

Vostok I.   Caroline I.

Eiao
Nuku Hiva   Ua Huka
1260

N

Marquesas
Islands

iulakita

Manihiki
Atoll

Tahuata

Fatu Hiva

Swains I.

Nassau

Flint I.

Napuka

Wallis Is.   Savai'i   Samoa
Upolu   Tutuila   Rose

Suvarrow A.

Rangiroa   Manihi
Mataiva   Apataki

Pukapuka

anua Levu   Nua

Lau Group
Vava'u Gr.

Society Is.
Bora Bora
Maupihaa   Raiatea

Fakarava   Raroia
Anaa   Makemo
224f   Hao

Tangatau

Takakoto

Palmerston A.

Aitutaki A.
Hervey Is.

Tahiti

Nengonengo   Reo

Marokau   Pukarua

Ha'apai   Tonga
Group (Friendly Is.)

Beveridge Reef

Hereherelue

Pinaki

Eua I.

Rarotonga

Is.Duc de   Tureia
Gloucester

10882

Mangaia

Is.Maria

Rurutu

Tematangi
Rimatara   Tubuai
Raivavae   Mururoa   Marutea
Mangareva

Tubuai Is.
(Austral Is.)

Gambier Is.   Oeno I.

Morane

Tropic of Capricorn

Raoul I.

Haymet Rfs.

Neilson Reef

Rapa

Pitcairn I.

Henderson I.

Ducie I.

auley I.
10047
tis I.

Kermadec Is.

Ilots de Bass
(Morotiri)

1088

th Island

Southwest

6600

Pacific

290   Chatham Is.

Basin

6010

Copyright: Vallardi Ind. Graf.

ALTITUDES		
	Metres	
	Feet	
	4000	13123
	3000	9843
	2000	6562
	1000	3281
	500	1640
	200	656
Sea level	0	
	Depression	
DEPTHS	0	
	200	656
	2000	6562
	4000	13123
	6000	19685
	More than	

55

The extensive pasturelands in most parts of the Australian continent are the unlimited kingdom of sheep and cattle. In the early 1970s there were 140 million sheep in Australia, more than in any other country in the world. The fine wool of the merino sheep is particularly prized. Australian production of wool amounts to about one-quarter of total world production. And with nearly 30 million cattle, Australia ranks as one of the leading beef-producing nations.

When the settlers brought sheep and cattle to Australia, they also brought rabbits with them. Once these attained their freedom, they were able to breed undisturbed in the boundless grazing country. Soon they constituted a plague on the land. As they ate all the grass right down to the roots, whole expanses of pastureland were destroyed. In the 1950s, almost all the 750 million rabbits were exterminated by a disease called myxomatosis, but the few who survived were immune to the virus that was meant to destroy them. Since then, they have multiplied again, and as yet no new remedy has been found to combat this menace.

Tarawa (pop. 11,000).

Formerly a protectorate, these islands are now a British colony administered by a governor. The country comprises 42 coral atolls spread over some 2 million square miles (5 million sq km) of the Pacific, stretching across the equator just west of the International Date Line. Most of the atolls rise to no more than 12 feet (3.5 metres) above sea level, and are thickly wooded with coconut palms. More than four-fifths of the people are Micronesians and live on the Gilbert group. About a seventh are Polynesians and live on the Ellice group. Ocean Island, to the west of the Gilbert group, has important phosphate deposits. The only other export is copra.

GUAM Area 209 sq miles (541 sq km); population 105,000; capital, Agaña (pop. 2,000).

The largest of the Mariana Islands, in the North Pacific, Guam was acquired by the United States from Spain in 1898. It was granted statutory powers of self-government in 1950, and the people became US citizens. Most Guamanians are Chamorros (of Indonesian and Spanish descent). The island is of vital strategic importance as an air and naval base, and about a third of the inhabitants are military personnel and their families. The interior of Guam is mountainous, and coral reefs lie off the coast.

HAWAII Area 6,425 sq miles (16,641 sq km); population 832,000; capital, Honolulu (pop. 325,000).

A group of islands in the central Pacific, about 2,400 miles (3,860 km) west of the US mainland, Hawaii was accepted as the 50th state of the United States in 1959. It had been a US territory since 1900. The group comprises a 1,610-mile (2,591-km) chain of 122 islands formed by volcanoes built up from the ocean floor. Of the eight main islands, located in the south-east, seven are inhabited. They have a mild climate and fertile soil. The largest island is called Hawaii and covers nearly two-thirds of the total area. It has two active volcanoes (Mauna Loa and Kilauea) and the highest peak in the state, Mauna Kea, which rises 13,796 feet (4,205 metres). About 80 per cent of Hawaii's inhabitants live on Oahu, the third largest island on which Honolulu and Pearl Harbor are located.

The original inhabitants of these islands were Polynesians, and 15 per cent of today's population have predominant Hawaiian ancestry. About 40 per cent are of White descent, and 30 per cent have Japanese ancestry. The chief products are cane-sugar and tropical fruits. About 35 per cent of the world's tinned pineapple is produced in Hawaii. The tourist industry is one of the state's largest sources of income.

NAURU Area 8 sq miles (21 sq km); population 7,000; capital, Nauru; currency, dollar (Australian); official languages, Nauruan and English.

A tiny island in the Pacific Ocean, Nauru became an independent republic in 1968, having a special relationship with the Commonwealth. It had been under German control from 1888 to 1914, when it surrendered to Australian forces. It was administered under a mandate until 1947 and then a trusteeship. It lies almost on the equator, north of New Zealand, and is surrounded by a coral reef.

Left: Australian Aborigines. When the first Englishmen stepped onto Australian soil they found an almost uninhabited continent. There were only an estimated 300,000 Aborigines, living as nomads, split up into a number of tribes, and unacquainted with either agriculture or cattle-rearing. They were, nevertheless, a peaceful people and did not oppose the advance of the White settlers. Today, the Aborigines have been confined to reservations, and there are plans for their eventual assimilation. Disease and unsuitable conditions of life, however, have reduced their numbers to about 100,000. Many of them still live as nomads, putting up leaf huts and simple windbreaks for shelter.

Right: A Polynesian fisherman, with a primitive form of harpoon. The Polynesians are a sea-loving race and the men are particularly skilled at catching fish, by any of several means—with fish-hooks, bent nails, rods, or nets. They are a tall, good-looking, light-skinned people, gay and carefree.

Its importance is due to its valuable deposits of phosphates. About half the people are Nauruans, a quarter are other Pacific islanders, and the rest are Chinese or European.

NEW CALEDONIA *Area 7,375 sq miles (19,103 sq km); population 130,000; capital, Nouméa (pop. 50,000).*

An island in the western Pacific 700 miles (1,127 km) east of Queensland, New Caledonia was annexed by France in 1853, and with its various island dependencies is an Overseas Territory of France. Nearly a half of the inhabitants are Melanesians, and a third are Europeans (mostly French). The island is rich in mineral resources, and is the third largest source of nickel in the world, after CAnada and the USSR. Chrome and iron deposits also abound, and various other minerals are mined.

NEW HEBRIDES *Area 5,700 sq miles (14,800 sq km); population 89,000; capital, Vila (pop. 6,000).*

A group of islands in the South Pacific some 500 miles (800 km) west of Fiji, the New Hebrides are administered by a unique Anglo-French Condominium. There are many active volcanoes on the islands. Most of the people are Melanesians. The chief product is copra.

NEW ZEALAND *Area 103,736 sq miles (268,675 sq km); population 2,910,000; capital, Wellington (pop. 329,000); currency, dollar (100 cents); official language, English.*

Like Australia, New Zealand is an independent parliamentary democracy on the British model. The head of state is the British monarch, represented by the governor-general. The country became a British colony in 1840 when the Maoris, the original native population, ceded sovereignty to the British Crown, and a dominion in 1907.

North and South Islands, which make up nearly 99 per cent of the territory of New Zealand, lie in the South Pacific, about 1,200 miles (1,930 km) east of Australia. There are a number of smaller islands, and New Zealand has responsibility for a large area in the Antarctic Ocean. North and South Islands are separated by Cook Strait, just 16 miles (26 km) wide. Much of the country is mountainous. The highest point, Mount Cook, rises 12,349 feet (3,764 metres) in the Southern Alps, which extend along the entire length of the South Island. There are several volcanoes, including two active ones, on the North Island, which is also noted for its hot springs and geysers. The countryside has great natural beauty and there are many lakes. The climate is temperate, with a narrow annual range of temperature.

About half of the country is used for agriculture, and 90 per cent of the farmland is used for rearing sheep and cattle. New Zealand is the third largest sheep-rearing and wool-producing country in the world. The main crops are wheat, barley, and oats. Apart from wool and meat, the most important exports are butter and cheese. New Zealand has few mineral resources, the principal ones being coal and gold. The generation of energy is dependent on hydro-electric power provided by the numerous rushing streams.

The development of New Zealand since the 1870s has been marked by the successful integration of the native population with the European immigrants (mostly from Great Britain). The Maoris are a branch of the Polynesian race and make up about 8 per cent of the total population.

Above: Melanesia. A village in the Fiji Islands. Typical of the native villages of the Pacific islands, the huts are made of wood and leaves, and stand in a picturesque setting of green palm trees. The Pacific islands to the north and east of Australia may be divided into three groups: Micronesia (small islands); Melanesia (black islands), for the population have dark skins; the third group is called Polynesia (many islands), as embracing a large number of far-flung islands.

Right centre: Two Australian Aborigines bedecked for a feast. The Aborigines have scarcely mixed with the European immigrants. There are few of them left, and they live in conditions similar to those of Stone Age man. They are beachcombers and hunters. It is the job of the women and children to gather tubers of all kinds. They also collect snails and other molluscs, and catch lizards, caterpillars, and snakes, which they prize highly as an item of food. The men trap kangaroos and emus, and smoke the opossum out of its den. Their weapons are coarsely worked stones, but they also use their famous boomerang—a good throw will carry this 600 feet (200 metres).

Right: The kangaroo. The first settlers in Australia could not believe their eyes when they saw so many remarkable animals—animals that are found only on the Australian continent. There are, for example, lungfishes that can breathe even in times of drought, because they possess a lung-like air-bladder; the bird world is extremely varied, and the fabulous appearance of the lyrebird is particularly exotic; but the most remarkable animal of all is still the kangaroo, not only because of the mighty leaps that it takes, but above all for its pouch, in which it nourishes its young.

Above: The outrigger canoe is used by the Polynesians for fishing and for travelling. This type of boat was an improvement on the dug-out. The outrigger has a counterbalance that makes it much more stable, so that men can take their families and stocks of food for quite long journeys on the stormy seas.

Below: A volcanic island in Polynesia. The islands of Polynesia are extraordinarily varied, and they are also distinguishable by their origin. The mountainous islands, such as Tahiti and Hawaii, are of volcanic origin. They are the peaks of subterranean mountain ranges, very common in Polynesia. Most of the small flat islands are coral reefs and atolls.

handed over control of British New Guinea in 1906 to Australia, who renamed it Papua, and the Australians also gained control of the German territory in 1921. They established joint control of the Territory of Papua and New Guinea in 1949. Among the more important of the other islands belonging to the country are New Britain and New Ireland, both in the Bismarck Archipelago.

Papua New Guinea lies wholly within the tropics, separated from Australia by the Torres Strait. A massive chain of mountain ranges stretches across the mainland, reaching a height of 15,400 feet (4,700 metres) with Mount Wilhelm in the Bismarck Range. The land is varied, with deep, forested valleys, large rivers and hundreds of swiftly flowing streams, and, to the south, one of the most extensive areas of swamp land in the world, extending into West Irian.

Most of the people are Melanesians, but there are also large groups of Papuans and Negritos. Farming is the principal occupation, and the chief crops are coffee, copra, and cocoa. Rubber and timber are also leading exports, and a copper mine on the island of Bougainville is proving a considerable source of revenue.

PAPUA NEW GUINEA *Area 178,000 sq miles (461,000 sq km); population 2,527,000; capital, Port Moresby (pop. 77,000); currency, dollar (Australian); official language, English.*

Formerly a dependency of Australia, Papua New Guinea became self-governing in 1973 and fully independent in 1975. The country comprises the eastern half of the island of New Guinea (West Irian, part of Indonesia, is the other half) and a number of islands off the northern and eastern coasts. Papua, the southern part of the eastern half of New Guinea, was annexed by Queensland in 1883 and became a British protectorate in 1884. The Germans took possession of the northern part in the same year. The British government

SAMOA, AMERICAN *Area 76 sq miles (197 sq km); population 28,000; capital, Pago Pago (pop. 2,000).*

This group of five volcanic islands and two coral atolls in the South Pacific has been a territory of the United States since 1900. The people are Polynesians and are US nationals. The chief products are tuna fish and copra.

SOLOMON ISLANDS *Area 11,500 sq miles (30,000 sq km); population 161,000; capital, Honiara (pop. 11,000).*

A British protectorate, the island group lies in the South Pacific to the east of Papua New Guinea. The larger islands are mountainous and forested, with rivers that tend to flood. The largest island is Guadalcanal. Most of the people are Melanesians. The chief exports are copra, timber, and fish.

TONGA *Area 270 sq miles (700 sq km); population 92,000; capital, Nuku'alofa (pop. 20,000); currency, pa'anga (100 seniti); official languages, English and Tongan.*

A British-protected state since 1900, Tonga became independent in 1970. The kingdom consists of 169 islands, which lie in the South Pacific just east of Fiji. They are also known as the Friendly Islands. Most of the islands are coral, but some are volcanic. Farming is the main occupation of the people, who are Polynesians, and copra and bananas are the chief exports. The tourist industry is being developed.

WESTERN SAMOA *Area 1,097 sq miles (2,842 sq km); population 131,000; capital, Apia (pop. 25,000); currency, tala (100 sene); official languages, English and Samoan.*

A German protectorate in the early 1900s, Western Samoa was administered by New Zealand from 1920 to 1961, before voting its own independence as from 1962. The country comprises 9 of the 14 islands of the Samoan Archipelago (the others constituting American Samoa). The two large islands, Savaii and Upolu, make up 99·8 per cent of Western Samoa's land area. They are mountainous, with rugged interiors. Most of the people, who are Polynesians, live in the coastal zones. The chief exports are copra, cocoa, and bananas.

POLAR REGIONS

The Polar regions are the areas surrounding the North and South Poles of the globe. Around the North Pole lies the Arctic. The Antarctic is centred at the South Pole. At the two Poles, the sun does not rise for six months in the year, while for the other six months it does not set. Both Polar regions have similar hard climatic conditions, but differ materially from each other in other respects. The Arctic is a sea surrounded by three continents, whereas the Antarctic consists basically of a mainland (Antarctica) surrounded by three oceans.

The North Polar Sea is a huge sea basin, covered mostly by pack-ice and drifting ice floes. The islands on its borders belong to Europe, Asia, and America. In these unproductive regions live several tens of thousands of people: the Lapps in Europe and the Eskimoes in America and Asia. These two ethnic groups belong to the Mongolian races. They still live mainly from their hunting and fishing.

Antarctica, on the other hand, is a gigantic highland region with an area of some 6 million square miles (15.5 million sq. km), or roughly twice the size of Australia. Icy winds sweep over the Antarctic mountains, which are on average 6,500 feet (2,000 metres) high, though the highest peak reaches over 16,000 feet (5,000 metres). This high plateau is covered with a thick layer of inland ice, pushing against the pack-ice at the edges into the three oceans that surround it. The South Polar region is completely uninhabited, except for the crews of the meteorological stations, which are of great scientific importance.

The story of polar exploration is a heroic and dramatic chapter in modern history. After many men had tried, the polar explorer Robert Peary planted the Stars and Stripes on the North Pole in 1909. Two years later, the Norwegian Roald Amundsen reached the South Pole, just five weeks before the tragic British expedition under Robert Scott achieved that goal, never to return. The American explorer Richard Byrd was the first man to fly over the North Pole (1926) and the South Pole (1929). Now airlines regularly fly over the northern polar route.

THE ANTARCTIC — Countless penguins live on the coast
THE ARCTIC — There are still Eskimoes living in igloos

59

ARCTIC REGIONS

ALTITUDES
Metres   Feet
3000   9843
1500   4921
500   1640
200   656
0

DEPTHS
0
200   656
1000   3281
2000   6562
3000   9843
More than

PACIFIC OCEAN

Aleutian Islands
Andreanof Is.   Rat Is.   Near Is.   Kuril Islands   Urup I.   Iturup I.   Hokkaido

C.Lopatka
Komandorskije Is   Paramushir I.   La Pérouse Str.   Sea of Japan

Unimak I.   Petropavlovsk-Kamchatski
Pribilof Is.   Mt.4850 Klyuchevsk   Sakhalin

Kodiak I.   St.Matthew I.   Bering Sea   Okhotsk   Nikolayevsk
Bristol Bay   C.Navarin   Kamchatka Pen.   Shelekhov Gulf   Amur

G.of Alaska   Nunivak I.   Gulf of Anadyr   Anadyr   Magadan   Shantar Is.
Seward   Norton Sound   Bering Strait   Koryak Ra.   Okhotsk   Dzhugdzhur Ra.
Queen Charlotte Islands   Nome   Chukchee Pen.   Gydan Ra. (Kolyma)   Stanovoy Ra.
Alexander Archipelago   Fotzebue   Chukot Ra.   UNION OF   Cherskiy Ra.
Juneau   Alaska Ra.   Mt.McKinley 6196   De Long Str.   Nizhne Kolymsk   Verkhoyansk Ra.
Coast Range   6050   Alaska (U.S.A.)   Wrangel I.   Kolyma   Yakutsk
Rocky Mountains   Fairbanks   Brooks Ra.   Bear Is.   Indigirka   Aldan
Fort Liard   Dawson   Barrow   Verkhoyansk   Vilyuy
Ft.McPherson   2816   C.Barrow   Kazache   SOVIET   Vilyuysk   Vitim
Peace   Mackenzie Mts.   Beaufort   New Siberia   Lyakhov Is.   Lena
Great Bear Lake   Sea   De Long Is.   Kotelny I.   Tiksi   Olenek   Lena
Great Slave Lake   New Siberian Islands   SOCIALIST   Olenek   Lomet
L.Athabasca   Amundsen Gulf   Banks I.   Lapten Sea   Nordvik   Tunguska
Dubarant L.   Victoria I.   McClure Str.   Pr.Patrick I.   C.Chelyuskin   REPUBLICS   Surgut
Churchill   L.Garry   King William I.   Melville I.   Borden I.   Bolshevik I.   Taimyr Pen.   Dudinka   Yenisey
Hudson   Prince of Wales I.   Queen Elizabeth   Sverdrup Is.   Severnaya Zemlya   L.Taimyr   Gyda   Ob
Southampton I.   Boothia Pen.   Islands   A.Heiberg I.   ARCTIC   October Revolution I.   Gyda Pen.   Salekhard   Surgut
Melville Pen.   Somerset I.   Devon I.   North Pole   Komsomolets I.   Yenisey   Yamal Pen.   Irtish   Tobolsk
Foxe Basin   Brodeur Pen.   Ellesmere I.   OCEAN   Franz Josef Land   Graham Bell I.   Bely I.   Ob   1894 Narodnaya
Foxe Pen.   Bylot I.   Smith Sd.   Wilczek Ld.   Gulf of Ob   Ural Mountains
Baffin Island   Thule   80   North East   George Land   Novaya Zemlya   Kara Sea
Hudson Strait   Baffin Bay   Land   Alexandra Ld.   Kolguyev I.   Yaman Tau 1638
Netilling L.   West Spitsbergen   Barents Sea   Kanin Pen.
Cumberland Peninsula   Peary Ld.   Spitsbergen   Pechora   Arkhangelsk   Kama
Ungava Bay   Disko I.   Greenland   Shannon   Greenland Sea   Bear I.   Kola Pen.   N.Dvina   Narodnaya
C.Chidley   2941   Kg.Christian x Ld.   Jan Mayen   North C.   Inari   Onega   L.Onega   Kazan
Davis Strait   King Christian IX Ld.   Scoresby Sd.   Murmansk   Lapland   Volga
King Frederik VI Ld.   Mt.Forel 3360   Denmark Strait   Narvik   Whitesea   Gorki   Kuybyshev
Frederikshaab   Angmagssalik   Arctic Circle   Lofoten Is.   70   Luleå   Ladoga   Volga
C.Farewell   Norwegian Sea   Trondheim   Umeå   Onega
Reykjavik   Oraefajökull 2119   Jan Mayen   2481   Helsinki   Estonia   L.Onega
ICELAND   Faeroe Is.   Oslo   Stockholm   Riga   Latvia   Lithuania   Kaliningrad
Rockall   Shetland Is.   60   Bergen   Gotland   Åland   Vienna
ATLANTIC OCEAN   Orkney Is.   North Sea   Copenhagen   Gdansk   Warsaw
British Isles   Scotland   DENMARK   Hamburg   POLAND
Dublin   Glasgow   GREAT   Berlin   Oder   Prague
IRELAND   England   Great Sea   W.GER.   E.GER.   CZECHOSLOVAKIA
BRITAIN   London   BELGIUM   Bonn   Danube
St.George's Ch.   English Channel   LUX.   Munich   AUSTRIA HUNGARY
South Limit of Drift Ice   Le Havre   FRANCE

North Pole   80

Beaufort Sea   80

ARCTIC OCEAN   80

Barents Sea

Scale 1:30 000 000
0   250   500   750   1000   1250   1500 Kms.
250   500   750   1000 St.mls.

Itineraries of the main Arctic expeditions
- – – – Peary-1908-1909
- –·–·– Amundsen-Nobile (Norwegian) -1926
- ········ Byrd-1926
- ———— Nobile-1928
- ———— Limit of the inhabited areas

SPITZBERGEN inset
Sjuöyane   C.Platen   C.Smith
North C.   White I.
Dansköya   Moffen   Storöya
Haakon VII Land   Hinlopen Strait   North-East Land
Ny Alesund   1717   C.Mohr   King Karl Land
Prins Karls Forland   432   Newton   Kelöya
1280   West Spitsbergen   Olga Strait   Kongsöya
Is.Fjorden   Barents   Svenskeöya
Bell Sund   610   Edge
Storr   491   Forell I.
3439   Negerpynten
C.South

SPITZBERGEN
Scale 1:10 000 000
0   50   100   150   200 Kms.

Copyright: Vallardi Ind.Graf.

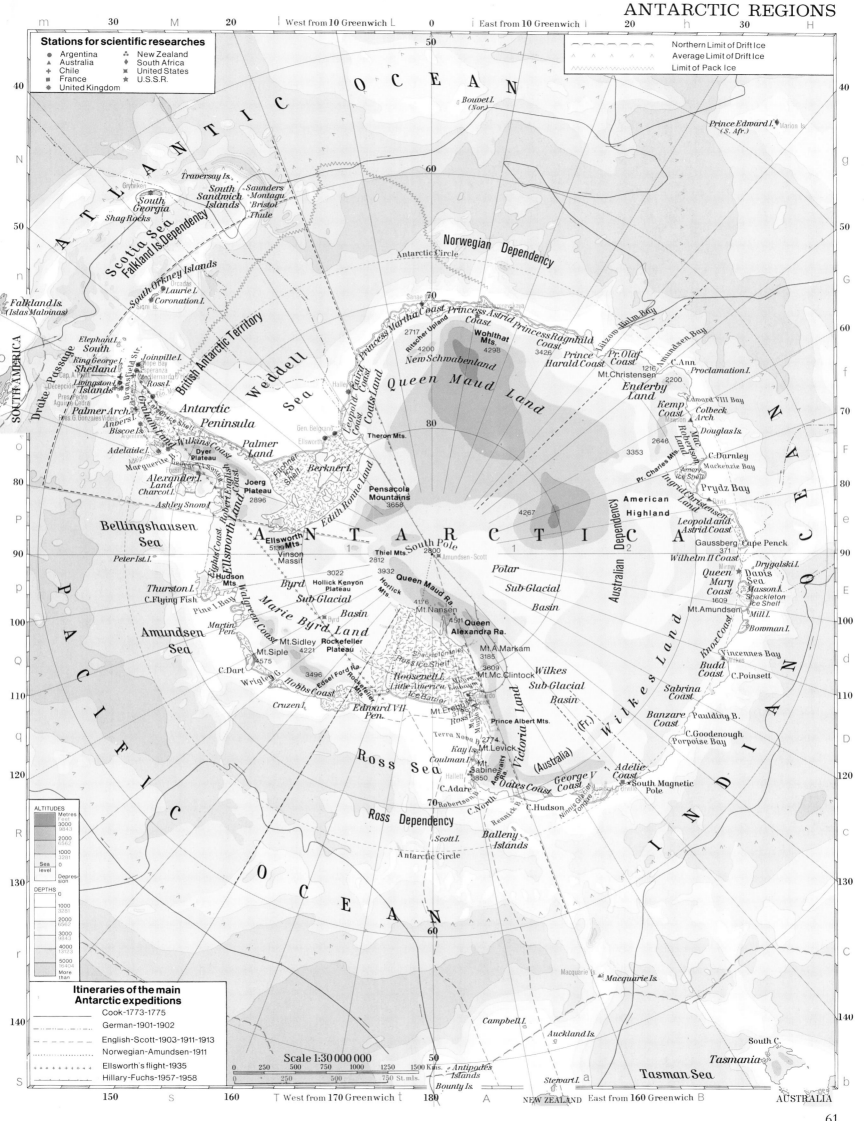

ANTARCTIC REGIONS

Northern Limit of Drift Ice
Average Limit of Drift Ice
Limit of Pack Ice

Stations for scientific researches

- Argentina
- Australia
- Chile
- France
- United Kingdom
- New Zealand
- South Africa
- United States
- U.S.S.R.

Itineraries of the main Antarctic expeditions

- Cook-1773-1775
- German-1901-1902
- English-Scott-1903-1911-1913
- Norwegian-Amundsen-1911
- Ellsworth's flight-1935
- Hillary-Fuchs-1957-1958

ATLANTIC OCEAN

Bouvet I. (Nor.)

Prince Edward I. (S. Afr.) Marion Is.

Traversay Is.

Grytviken South Sandwich Islands Saunders Montagu Bristol Thule

South Georgia

Shag Rocks

Norwegian Dependency

Antarctic Circle

Sanae 70 Princess Astrid Coast Princess Ragnhild Coast

Princess Martha Coast

Nivostokovaya

Atkazow Holm Bay

Amundsen Bay

Falkland Is. Dependency

Scotia Sea

South Orkney Islands

Orcadas Laurie I. Coronation I.

Signi Is.

Elephant I. South Shetland Islands

King George I. Joinville I. Hope Bay Esperanza

Cap. A. Prat San Bernardo Ross I. Ferraz

Deception Livingston I.

Pres. Pedro Aguirre Cedra

Palmer Arch.

Ritscher Upland 2717 Wohlthat Mts. 4298

New Schwabenland 4200 Queen Maud Land 3426 Prince Harald Coast Pr. Olaf Coast

Mt. Christensen 1216 C. Ann Proclamation I.

Enderby Land 2200

British Antarctic Territory

Weddell Sea

Princess Elizabeth Land

Caird Coast Coats Land

Halley Gen. Belgrano Ellsworth Theron Mts.

Kemp Coast Edward VIII Bay

Mac Robertson Land Mawson

Colbeck Arch Douglas Is.

Antarctic Peninsula

Graham Land

Wilkins Coast

Dyer Plateau

Palmer Land

Fitchner Ice Shelf Berkner I.

2646 3353 C. Darnley Mackenzie Bay

Pr. Charles Mts. Amery Ice Shelf

Ingrid Christensen Land

Adelaide I. Adelaide

Marguerite George VI Sound

Alexander I. Land Charcot I.

Joerg Plateau 2896

Pensacola Mountains 3658

Prydz Bay Davis

American Highland 4267

Leopold and Astrid Coast

Gaussberg 371 Cape Penck

Wilhelm II Coast

Ashley Snow

Bellingshausen Sea

Edith Ronne Land

Ellsworth Mts. 5139

Vinson Massif

Thiel Mts. 2812 South Pole 2800

Amundsen-Scott

Polar

Sub-Glacial

Australian Dependency

Drygalski I.

Queen Mary Coast Davis Sea Masson I. 1609 Shackleton Ice Shelf

Mill I.

Peter Ist. I.

Hudson Mts.

Byrd 3022 Hollick Kenyon Plateau Horlick Mts. 3932 Queen Maud Ra. 4176

Sub-Glacial Basin

Mt. Amundsen Bowman I.

Thurston I. C. Flying Fish Pine I. Bay

Byrd

Martin Pen.

Marie Byrd Land

Mt. Nansen 4511 Queen Alexandra Ra.

Knox Coast Vincennes Bay Wilkes Budd Coast C. Poinsett

PACIFIC OCEAN

Amundsen Sea

Mt. Sidley Mt. Siple 4221 4575

C. Dart

Wrigley G. Hobbs Coast

Cruzen I.

Rockefeller Plateau

Edsel Ford Ra. Rockefeller Mts. 3496

Edward VII Pen.

Shackleton Inlet

Roosevelt I. Ross Ice Shelf Little America Ice Barrier

Mt. A. Markam 3185

Mt. Mc.Clintock 3609

Wilkes Sub-Glacial Basin

Sabrina Coast

Banzare Coast Paulding B.

C. Goodenough Porpoise Bay

Victoria Land

Mt. Erebus Ross I.

Prince Albert Mts.

Terra Nova B. 2774 Mt. Levick

Kay Is.

Coulman I.

(Fr.) Adélie Coast

George V Coast South Magnetic Pole

Ross Sea

Ninnis Glacier Tongue

C. Adare Mt. Sabine 3850 Admiralty Ra.

Hallett C. North

Oates Coast

C. Hudson

D'Urville

Ross Dependency

Robertson B. Rennick B.

Scott I.

Balleny Islands

Antarctic Circle

INDIAN OCEAN

Macquarie Is.

Campbell I.

Auckland Is.

South C.

NEW ZEALAND

AUSTRALIA

Tasman Sea

Tasmania

Scale 1:30 000 000

0 250 500 750 1000 1250 1500 Kms.
0 250 500 750 St. mls.

Antipodes Islands

Bounty Is. Stewart I.

ALTITUDES

Metres	Feet
3000	9843
2000	6562
1000	3281
Sea level	0
Depression	

DEPTHS

0	
1000	3281
2000	6562
3000	9843
4000	13123
5000	16404
More than	

61

INDEX

INDEX OF COUNTRIES